HIGH SCHOOL GRAMMAR WORKBOOK GRADE 9-12

GRAMMAR PRACTICE WORKBOOK HIGH SCHOOL: ACHIEVE HIGHER TEST SCORES WITH INTERACTIVE EXERCISES

SAT ACT

A+

DR. FANATOMY

★★★★★

Bonus Booklet For You!

With great pleasure, I warmly welcome you to purchase the book. Congratulations on stepping towards improving yourself and developing the skills necessary to thrive as a teenager and beyond.

Below is a surprise gift for you!

Download it from the link (or scan the QR code below)
https://bit.ly/TeeNavigationBonus

TABLE OF CONTENTS

Subject-Verb Agreement
- *Singular vs. plural subjects and verbs*
- *Common subject-verb agreement challenges*

Sentence Fragments and Run-ons
- *How to avoid and fix fragments*
- *Correcting run-on sentences*

Parallel Structure
- Maintaining parallelism in lists and comparisons
- Exercises to improve sentence balance

Trivia Corner

Activity Corner 3

4. PUNCTUATION AND CAPITALIZATION

End Marks: Periods, Question Marks, and Exclamation Points
- *Proper use of end punctuation*
- *Common errors and how to fix them*

Commas
- *Comma usage in lists, compound sentences, after introductory elements, and with nonessential clauses*

Semicolons and Colons
- *Connecting related independent clauses*
- *Introducing lists or emphasizing information*

Quotation Marks and Dialogue
- *Correct formatting of dialogue*
- *Using quotation marks for quotes, titles, and special cases*

Apostrophes
- *Possessive nouns and contractions*
- *Common errors with apostrophes*

Capitalization Rules

- *Proper nouns, titles, and sentence beginnings*
- *Avoiding capitalization mistakes*

Trivia Corner

Activity Corner 4

5. PRONOUNS AND THEIR CORRECT USAGE

Types of Pronouns

- *Personal, relative, reflexive, indefinite, demonstrative pronouns*

Pronoun-Antecedent Agreement
- *Ensuring pronouns match their antecedents in number and gender*

Avoiding Vague Pronoun References
- *Clarifying ambiguous pronouns in sentences*

Appositive and Prepositional Phrases
- Enhancing sentences with appositive phrases
- Correct use of prepositional phrases in writing

Trivia Corner

Activity Corner 8

Eliminating Wordiness
- *How to be concise in writing without losing meaning*

Avoiding Clichés and Redundancies
- *Identifying and revising common clichés and redundant phrases*

Improving Sentence Variety
- *Using a mix of sentence structures to create engaging writing*

Transitions and Flow
- *Using transitions effectively to maintain a logical flow between ideas*

Trivia Corner

Activity Corner 9

Double Negatives

Confusing Words and Homophones

Tricks for Confusing Words

Common Spelling and Grammar Mistakes

Tips for Avoiding Common Mistakes

Trivia Corner

Activity Corner 10

- *Additional Resources*

1.   Introduction to Grammar

What is Grammar?

Grammar comprises the rules that govern how we construct sentences and communicate ideas. It's akin to the foundation of a building - without a sturdy structure, everything collapses. Likewise, your writing can become ambiguous or perplexing without correct grammar.

Importance of Grammar in Writing and Communication

Having good grammar is crucial for communicating effectively. Whether you're writing an essay for school, composing an email to a teacher, or even posting on social media, using proper grammar helps to ensure that your message is clear. People are more likely to understand and respect your message when it is grammatically correct.

Practical Example:

Imagine you're writing an email to a potential employer:

Incorrect: *I wants to apply for the job. My skills is suitable for the position.*

Correct: *I want to apply for the job. My skills are suitable for the position.*

In the incorrect sentence, "wants" and "is" are used improperly, which could make a poor impression on the employer. Using "want" and "are" makes the message clear and professional.

How Grammar Affects Test Scores (SAT, ACT, etc.)

Grammar is crucial in standardized tests such as the SAT and ACT. Multiple sections of these tests necessitate the correction of grammatical errors and the enhancement of sentence structure. Proficiency in grammar can enhance your test scores and increase your chances of getting into your preferred college.

Example SAT-style Question: Choose the correct form of the verb:

The students *is/are* excited about the upcoming project.

Answer: are

Explanation: "Students" is a plural noun, so it requires the plural form of the verb "are."

Overview of Grammar Components

Grammar is made up of several key components. Understanding each one helps you write with greater clarity and precision.

Parts of Speech

Here's a breakdown of the eight parts of speech:

- **Nouns**: Names a person, place, thing, or idea. Example: John, school, book, happiness

- **Pronouns**: Words that replace nouns. Example: he, she, it, they

- **Verbs:** Words that describe actions or states. Example: run, swim, think, is

- **Adjectives**: Words that describe nouns. Example: big, blue, fast

- **Adverbs**: Words that modify verbs, adjectives, or other adverbs. Example: quickly, very, happily

- **Conjunctions:** Words that connect clauses or sentences. Example: and, but, because

- **Prepositions**: Words that show the relationship between a noun and another word. Example: in, on, under

- **Interjections**: Words that express strong emotion. Example: Wow!, Oops!, Hey!

Table of Parts of Speech with Examples:

Part of Speech	Definition	Example
Noun	Person, place, thing, or idea	student, library, joy
Pronoun	Replaces a noun	he, she, they
Verb	Action or state	run, is, think
Adjective	Describes a noun	red, smart, fast
Adverb	Describes a verb, adjective, or adverb	quickly, softly, extremely
Conjunction	Connects clauses	and, but, or *for and, nor, but, or, yet, so FANBOYS (acronym)*
Preposition	Shows relationships *connects the noun to the verb (filler sentences)*	on, in, above *in the*
Interjection	Expresses emotion */feelings*	Wow!, Hey!, Ouch!

Practical Exercise:

Identify the parts of speech in the following sentence:

The dog quickly ran to the park because it saw a squirrel.

Answer:
- Noun: dog, park, squirrel
- Adverb: quickly
- Verb: ran, saw
- Conjunction: because
- Pronoun: it

How Grammar Rules Impact Writing

Grammar rules provide structure to your writing. Without them, even the best ideas can become confusing.

Clarity and Readability
Good grammar makes your writing clear and easy to understand.

7

When grammar rules are ignored, the message becomes unclear, which can frustrate or confuse the reader.

Example:

Incorrect: *The teacher gave the homework to the students that were difficult.*

Correct: *The teacher gave the difficult homework to the students.*

In the incorrect sentence, it sounds like the students are difficult. The correct sentence clarifies that it's the homework that is difficult.

Common Errors in Everyday Writing Some common grammar mistakes include:

- **Run-On Sentences:** Combining too many ideas into one sentence without proper punctuation.
  - **Incorrect**: I went to the store I bought some milk.
  - **Correct**: I went to the store, and I bought some milk.

- **Comma Splices:** Using a comma where a period or conjunction is needed.
  - **Incorrect**: She loves to read, she doesn't like writing.
  - **Correct**: She loves to read, but she doesn't like writing.

Table of Common Errors:

Error Type	Incorrect Example	Correct Example	Explanation
Run-On Sentence	I ran to the store I bought snacks.	I ran to the store, and I bought snacks.	A run-on sentence occurs when two or more independent clauses are joined without proper punctuation or conjunctions.
Comma Splice	I was hungry, I made a sandwich.	I was hungry, so I made a sandwich.	A comma splice happens when two independent clauses are incorrectly joined by a comma. Use a conjunction or separate them into two sentences.
Subject-Verb Agreement	The dog bark loudly.	The dog barks loudly.	The subject and verb must agree in number (singular or plural). In this case, "dog" is singular, so the verb should be "barks," not "bark."
Fragment	Because I was tired.	I went to bed early because I was tired.	A fragment is an incomplete sentence, missing a subject or verb. It doesn't express a complete thought.
Misplaced Modifier	She almost drove to the beach every day.	She drove to the beach almost every day.	Misplaced modifiers are words or phrases that are not placed correctly in relation to the word they modify, causing confusion.

Error Type	Incorrect Example	Correct Example	Explanation
Dangling Modifier	Walking through the park, the flowers were beautiful.	Walking through the park, I noticed the beautiful flowers.	A dangling modifier is a word or phrase that doesn't logically modify any word in the sentence. The sentence should clarify who is walking through the park.
Pronoun-Antecedent Agreement	Every student should bring their book.	Every student should bring his or her book.	The pronoun must agree with its antecedent in number and gender. "Student" is singular, so the pronoun should be "his or her," not "their."
Tense Shift	Yesterday, I go to the mall and bought a dress.	Yesterday, I went to the mall and bought a dress.	A tense shift occurs when the verb tense changes within the same sentence or paragraph without a clear reason. Use consistent verb tenses.
Double Negative	I don't have no money.	I don't have any money.	A double negative happens when two negative words are used in the same sentence, which makes the meaning unclear. One negative word should be used for clarity.
Parallelism	She likes reading, writing, and to swim.	She likes reading, writing, and swimming.	Parallelism ensures that items in a list or series are in the same grammatical form. In this case, all verbs should be in the "-ing" form.
Improper Pronoun Case	Him and me went to the concert.	He and I went to the concert.	Pronouns must be in the correct case. In this example, "Him and me" should be "He and I," since they are the subjects of the sentence.
Faulty Comparison	My car is faster than anyone in the race.	My car is faster than any other car in the race.	Faulty comparisons occur when the items being compared are unclear. In this case, it's unclear if the car is being compared to people or other cars.
Confusing Homophones	Their going to the store to buy some food.	They're going to the store to buy some food.	Homophones are words that sound alike but have different meanings. "Their" refers to possession, while "they're" is a contraction for "they are."
Pronoun Reference Ambiguity	When Sarah told Emily that she was accepted, she was excited.	When Sarah told Emily that she was accepted, Sarah was excited.	Ambiguous pronoun references occur when it's unclear which noun the pronoun refers to. Clarify by repeating the subject, if necessary.
Improper Use of Apostrophe	The dog lost it's collar.	The dog lost its collar.	Apostrophes show possession or contractions. "It's" is a contraction of "it is," while "its" shows possession. In this case, "its" is the correct form.
Inconsistent Point of View	One should take care of yourself.	One should take care of oneself.	Inconsistent point of view happens when the pronouns change within a sentence. Keep the pronouns consistent throughout.
Redundancy	I made a new invention.	I made an invention.	Redundancy occurs when unnecessary words or phrases are added to a sentence. "New" is implied in the word "invention," so it can be removed.
Incorrect Use of Prepositions	She was angry on her friend.	She was angry with her friend.	Prepositions can change the meaning of a sentence. In this case, "angry with" is the correct prepositional phrase.

Grammar and Standardized Testing

Standardized tests like the SAT, ACT, and high school exams place a strong emphasis on grammar. Here's how you can expect to see grammar tested.

SAT Writing and Language Section

The SAT tests your ability to identify grammatical mistakes in passages. These questions often involve subject-verb agreement, comma usage, and improving sentence structure.

ACT English Section

The ACT focuses on grammar, punctuation, sentence structure, and rhetorical skills. You'll be asked to correct errors and revise passages for clarity and flow.

Common Grammar Topics in Tests:

- **Verb Tense**: Making sure verbs agree in time (past, present, or future).
    - *Incorrect: He goes to the park yesterday.*
    - *Correct: He went to the park yesterday.*

- **Pronoun Clarity**: Ensuring pronouns clearly refer to the correct noun.
    - *Incorrect: When John met Bob, he was excited. (Who is "he"?)*
    - *Correct: When John met Bob, John was excited.*

Practical Example of a Grammar Test Question:
Original Sentence:

The group of students were going to the museum tomorrow.

Choose the correct form of the verb:
- a) was
- b) were
- c) is

Correct Answer: a) was

Explanation: Although "students" is plural, the subject is "group," which is singular, so the verb should be singular too: was.

Practical Activities to Reinforce Grammar Learning:

Activity 1: Grammar Correction

Rewrite the following sentences, correcting the grammar mistakes:
1. The team are playing well this season.
2. She don't like the new teacher.
3. They should of gone to the park instead.

Answers:
1. The team is playing well this season.
2. She doesn't like the new teacher.
3. They should have gone to the park instead.

Activity 2: Parts of Speech Challenge

In the following paragraph, underline the nouns, circle the verbs, and put a box around the adjectives.

The quick brown fox jumps over the lazy dog.

Here's how the parts of speech break down:

- *Nouns : fox, dog*
- *Verbs : jumps*
- *Adjectives : quick, brown, lazy*

TRIVIA CORNER

- *Greek Roots: The word "grammar" originates from the Greek word "grammatike," meaning "the art of letters."*

- *Shakespeare's Vocabulary: William Shakespeare coined over 1,700 words, expanding the English language with terms like "bedroom," "excitement," and "swagger."*

- *A Lungful of Letters: The longest word in the English language recognized in major dictionaries is "pneumonoultramicroscopicsilicovolcanoconiosis," a medical term for a lung disease.*

- *The Oxford Comma: This comma can clarify meaning. For example, "I love my parents, Beyoncé, and Justin Bieber" is different from "I love my parents, Beyoncé and Justin Bieber."*

- *Punctuation Powerhouse: English has 14 punctuation marks, including less common ones like the interrobang (‽) and the caret (^).*

- *Vowel-less Sentences: Grammatically correct sentences can exist without traditional vowels. "Shh, crypts fly by my spry gypsy" is an example.*

- *Shortest Sentence: "Go" is the shortest complete sentence in English, containing a subject (implied you) and a verb.*

- *The Most Common Letter: The letter "E" is the most frequently used letter in English.*

- *Palindromes: These words, phrases, or sentences read the same forward and backward, like "level," "racecar," and "A man, a plan, a canal, Panama!"*

- *"I" Love Myself: The personal pronoun "I" is the most commonly used word in English, reflecting our tendency to talk about ourselves.*

◎ ACTIVITY CORNER 1

Activity 1: Identify the Parts of Speech

Find out word in the sentence and label it with its part of speech (noun, verb, adjective, adverb, conjunction, preposition, pronoun, interjection).

Sentence:

"After school, Tim quickly ran to the park and played soccer with his friends."

- .... – *Verb*
- .... – *Preposition*
- ....– *Article (Adjective)*
- .... – *Noun*
- .... – *Conjunction*
- .... – *Verb*
- .... – *Noun*
- .... – *Preposition*
- .... – *Pronoun*
- .... – *Noun*

Activity 2: Correct the Common Grammar Errors

Identify and correct the grammar errors in the following sentences.

1. *Me and my friend is going to the mall.*
2. *She don't like broccoli.*
3. *They was late to class yesterday.*
4. *He could of went to the game, but he choosed to stay home.*

Activity 3: Fix the Sentence for Clarity

Rearrange or rewrite the following sentence to make it clearer and more grammatically correct.

Sentence:

"Running through the park, the trees looked beautiful."

ACTIVITY CORNER 1

Activity 4: Match the Grammar Component

Match the part of speech to its example.

Part of Speech	Example
1. Noun	a. Quickly
2. Verb	b. The
3. Adjective	c. Cat
4. Adverb	d. Beautiful
5. Pronoun	e. Ran
6. Preposition	f. She
7. Conjunction	g. With
8. Article	h. And

Activity 5 : SAT/ACT Grammar Practice

Choose the correct form of the verb or pronoun for the following sentence:

1. *Either the dog or the cats (is/are) making a mess in the yard.*
2. *Everyone (has/have) completed their homework for today.*
3. *Neither Sarah nor the other students (was/were) late to class.*
4. *Each of the players (is/are) responsible for bringing their own equipment.*

2. Parts of Speech

Understanding Parts of Speech

It is essential to understand the parts of speech to master grammar and improve writing and communication skills. This chapter will cover the fundamental parts of speech: nouns, pronouns, verbs, adjectives, adverbs, conjunctions, prepositions, and interjections. Each section includes examples, tables, and practice activities to help reinforce what you have learned.

Nouns and Pronouns :

Nouns are words that refer to people, places, things, or ideas. They form the foundation of sentences, naming the subjects and objects of action. There are various types of nouns, each with its own characteristics and usage. Understanding these types will enhance your ability to express yourself effectively and precisely.

Type of Noun	Definition	Example
Common Noun	A general name for a person, place, or thing	dog, city, car, book
Proper Noun	A specific name for a person, place, or thing (capitalized)	Michael, New York, Honda, Amazon
Abstract Noun	Names an idea, quality, or state	freedom, love, intelligence
Collective Noun	Refers to a group of people or things	team, class, flock, jury
Compound Noun	A noun made up of two or more words	basketball, mother-in-law, toothpaste

Examples in Sentences:

- **Common noun**: The **car** is parked outside the house.
- **Proper noun**: My best friend, **Sarah**, lives in **Paris**.
- **Abstract noun**: She values **honesty** in her relationships.
- **Collective noun**: The **jury** is ready to announce its decision.
- **Compound noun**: He plays **basketball** every weekend.

16

Pronouns are words used to replace nouns, preventing repetition and making sentences smoother.

Types of Pronouns:

Type	Definition	Example
Personal Pronouns	Replaces people or things	he, she, it, they
Possessive Pronouns	Show ownership	his, her, their, its
Reflexive Pronouns	Refers back to the subject	myself, yourself, themselves
Demonstrative Pronouns	Points to specific things	this, that, these, those
Relative Pronouns	Introduces dependent clauses	who, whom, which, that

Pronoun-Antecedent Agreement:

Pronouns must agree with their antecedents (the noun they replace) in both number (singular/plural) and gender.

Examples:

- *Incorrect: Each student should bring their book.*
- *Correct: Each student should bring his or her book.(Student is singular, so the pronoun must be singular.)*

Practice Example:

- The dog lost its ball.
- All the students brought their assignments.

The use of "its" and "their" in these sentences is appropriate because they refer to possessive pronouns of singular and plural nouns, respectively:

- "its" refers to "dog" (singular).
- "their" refers to "students" (plural).

Consistency in Verb Tense Usage:

- Incorrect: I was eating when he comes into the room.
- Correct: I was eating when he came into the room.

Adjectives and Adverbs

- **Adjectives** modify nouns and pronouns, giving more information about them.

- **Adverbs** modify verbs, adjectives, or other adverbs, explaining how, when, where, or to what extent something happens.

Modifier	Used to Describe	Examples
Adjective	Nouns or pronouns	The blue car, happy students
Adverb	Verbs, adjectives, or other adverbs	She sings beautifully, very fast car

Examples in Sentences:

- **Adjective:** The tall boy ran across the green field.
- **Adverb:** She quickly finished her homework.
- **Adverb modifying adjective:** The movie was extremely interesting.

Conjunctions, Prepositions, and Interjections

Conjunctions join words, phrases, or clauses in a sentence. There are three types:

Conjunction Type	Function	Example
Coordinating Conjunctions	Connects words, phrases, or independent clauses	and, but, or, so

18

Conjunction Type	Function	Example
Subordinating Conjunctions	Connects dependent clauses to independent clauses	because, although, since
Correlative Conjunctions	Pairs of conjunctions that work together	either...or, neither...nor

Examples in Sentences:

- *I wanted to go to the beach,* **but** *it started raining.*
- *She couldn't go out* **because** *she was sick.*
- *You can* **either** *take the bus* **or** *walk to school.*

Prepositions show relationships between nouns (or pronouns) and other words in a sentence, usually describing location, time, or direction.

Common Prepositions:

Preposition Type	Examples
Location	in, on, under, above, beside
Time	at, during, after, before
Direction	to, toward, through, into

Examples in Sentences:

- *The book is* **on** *the table.*
- *We arrived* **after** *the movie started.*

Interjections are words or phrases that express strong emotion or surprise. They are often followed by an exclamation mark.

Examples:
- **Wow!** *That was an amazing game.*
- **Oh no!** *I forgot my homework.*

Summary Table: Parts of Speech

Part of Speech	Function	Examples
Noun	Names a person, place, thing, or idea	dog, Sarah, happiness, team
Pronoun	Replaces a noun	he, she, it, they, who, his
Verb	Expresses action or state of being	run, jump, is, seem, have
Adjective	Describes or modifies a noun or pronoun	blue, tall, interesting
Adverb	Describes or modifies a verb, adjective, or other adverb	quickly, very, extremely
Conjunction	Connects words, phrases, or clauses	and, but, because, either...or
Preposition	Shows a relationship between a noun and another word	on, in, after, through
Interjection	Expresses emotion or surprise	Wow!, Oops!, Oh no!

Sample Question : Pronoun-Antecedent Agreement (SAT/ACT Style)

Question: Select the answer that correctly completes the sentence:

Each of the students brought (A) their, (B) his or her, (C) its, (D) they're materials to class.

Explanation: The pronoun must agree in number with its antecedent. "Each" is singular, so the correct pronoun must also be singular.

Correct Answer: B) his or her

Trivia Corner

- The word "noun" comes from the Latin word *nomen*, meaning "name." Every noun is essentially a label for something!

- The most commonly used noun in English is *time*. Can you guess the next two most used nouns? (Hint: *person* and *year*!)

- What's the longest word in English that can be typed using only the left hand on a standard keyboard? It's *stewardesses*, and it contains eight letters—all nouns!

- Pronouns like *I, you, he, she,* and *they* help avoid repetition. Imagine how awkward it would be to say, "John went to John's house, and John ate John's lunch."

- Verbs are the action words in a sentence. The word *verb* itself comes from the Latin word *verbum*, meaning "word," because verbs are considered the most important part of a sentence!

- Shakespeare was a master of language, creating over 1,700 new words! He even turned nouns into verbs, like *eyeball* and *gossip*.

- The adjective *unique* means "one of a kind." So, something can't be "more unique" or "most unique." It's either unique or it's not!

- There are over 500 prepositions in English, but only a handful are used most frequently. Can you name the five most common ones? (They're *of, in, to, for,* and *with*!)

- Conjunctions like *and, but,* and *or* are the glue that holds sentences together. They help connect different parts of a sentence smoothly.

- The interjection "Wow!" has been used to express surprise since at least the 16th century. It's one of the oldest interjections still in use today!

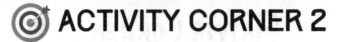 ACTIVITY CORNER 2

Activity 1: Identifying Types of Nouns

Identify whether the underlined nouns are proper, common, abstract, or collective

1. The **team** celebrated their victory after the match.
2. I can't wait to visit **Paris** this summer.
3. Her **bravery** during the storm was commendable.
4. A **flock** of birds flew across the sky.
5. **James** finished his homework before the deadline.

Activity 2 : Identifying Types of Nouns

Choose the correct pronoun to complete each sentence.

1. Each student should bring **(his or her / their)** notebook to class.
2. The dog chased **(its / their)** tail in circles.
3. Neither of the boys has done **(his / their)** homework yet.
4. Someone left **(his or her / their)** backpack in the hallway.
5. The committee made (its / their) final decision.

Activity 3: Verb Tense Consistency

Fill in the blanks with the correct verb tense to maintain consistency in each sentence.

1. Yesterday, I (walk) to the store, bought some groceries, and (cook) dinner.
2. By the time you arrive, we (finish) the project.
3. While she (study), her phone rang, and she (answer) it.
4. I (read) the book before I (watch) the movie.
5. Tomorrow, we (go) to the museum and (have) lunch.

ACTIVITY CORNER 2

Activity 4: Identifying Adjectives and Adverbs

Identify whether the bold words are adjectives or adverbs.

1. The **happy** children played in the park.
2. She sings **beautifully** at the school concert.
3. The **large** dog barked loudly at the strangers.
4. The train arrived **early** today.
5. They walked quietly through the library.

Activity 5 : Conjunctions and Prepositions

Fill in the blanks with the correct conjunction or preposition from the word bank. Use each word only once.

Word Bank: and, or, but, in, under

1. She waited ___ the tree for her friend.
2. We can go to the movies ___ get ice cream afterward.
3. He is very talented ___ also very humble.
4. I wanted to join the soccer team, ___ I was too late to sign up.
5. They placed the books ___ the shelf.

3. Sentence Structure

Sentence Structure

Understanding sentence structure is essential for improving your writing and communication skills. In this chapter, we will cover different types of sentences, master subject-verb agreement, learn how to avoid sentence fragments and run-ons and maintain parallel structure in your sentences. Each section contains examples, tables, and activities to help you fully understand these concepts.

Simple, Compound, and Complex Sentences :

Definitions:

Simple Sentence: A simple sentence has one independent clause with a subject and a verb. It expresses a complete thought.
- *Example: The students studied.*
- *Explanation: "Students" is the subject, and "studied" is the verb.*

Compound Sentence: A compound sentence contains two or more independent clauses joined by a coordinating conjunction (for, and, nor, but, or, yet, so).
- *Example: The students studied, and they passed the exam.*
- *Explanation: Two independent clauses ("The students studied" and "They passed the exam") joined by "and."*

Complex Sentence: A complex sentence contains one independent clause and one or more dependent (subordinate) clauses.
- *Example: Although the students studied hard, they found the exam difficult.*
- *Explanation: "Although the students studied hard" is a dependent clause, and "they found the exam difficult" is the independent clause.*

Examples of Sentence Types in Action:

Sentence Type	Example	Explanation
Simple Sentence	I completed the homework.	One independent clause.
Compound Sentence	I completed the homework, and I submitted it on time.	Two independent clauses joined by "and."
Complex Sentence	Because I completed the homework, I was able to relax.	One dependent clause ("Because I completed the homework") and one independent clause ("I was able to relax").

Using Varied Sentence Types in Writing:

Using a mix of simple, compound, and complex sentences can make your writing more dynamic and interesting.

- **Simple Sentences** provide clarity and punch. *Example: The teacher entered the room.*

- **Compound Sentences** connect related ideas. *Example: The teacher entered the room, and the students became silent.*

- **Complex Sentences** show cause and effect, conditions, or time relationships. *Example: When the teacher entered the room, the students became silent.*

Subject-Verb Agreement

Subject-verb agreement requires the subject and the verb in a sentence to match in number. If the subject is singular, the verb must be singular; if the subject is plural, the verb must be plural.

Singular Subject + Singular Verb:
- *Example: The cat runs fast.*
- *Explanation: "Cat" is singular, so "runs" is singular.*

Plural Subject + Plural Verb:
- *Example: The cats run fast.*
- *Explanation: "Cats" is plural, so "run" is plural.*

Tricky Subject-Verb Agreement Cases:

Subject Type	Sentence	Explanation
Indefinite Pronouns	Everyone is excited.	"Everyone" is singular, so we use "is."
Compound Subjects (joined by 'and')	My brother and sister are visiting.	"Brother and sister" is plural, so the verb is "are."
Subjects joined by 'or/nor'	Either the teacher or the students are wrong.	The verb agrees with the noun closer to it ("students" is plural, so "are").

Sentence Fragments and Run-ons

Sentence Fragments:

A sentence fragment is an incomplete sentence that lacks a subject, a verb, or a complete thought.

Fragment: Because I was late.

- *Why it's a fragment: It doesn't express a complete thought.*
- *Fix: Because I was late, I missed the bus.*

Run-On Sentences:

A run-on sentence occurs when two independent clauses are joined without proper punctuation or conjunctions.

- **Run-on: I love ice cream it's my favorite dessert.**

    - *Fix: I love ice cream, and it's my favorite dessert.*
    - *Alternative Fix: I love ice cream; it's my favorite dessert.*

Avoiding Sentence Fragments and Run-ons

Problem	Example	Correction
Fragment	Running through the park.	She was running through the park.
Run-on	He finished the test he was very tired.	He finished the test, and he was very tired.
Run-on (no punctuation)	I went to the store I bought bread.	I went to the store, and I bought bread.

Parallel Structure

Parallel structure, or parallelism, involves using the same grammatical pattern when creating a list or comparison in a sentence. This ensures that your writing is balanced and easy to read.

Parallelism in Lists:

When listing actions, items, or ideas, the format should stay consistent.

Incorrect: I like to read, running, and to swim.

- **Why it's wrong**: "To read" and "to swim" use the infinitive form, but "running" is a gerund (verb+ing).

Correct: I like reading, running, and swimming.

- **Why it's correct**: All three actions are in the gerund form (verb+ing).

Parallelism in Comparisons:

When comparing two or more things, both sides of the comparison should follow the same structure.

- **Incorrect:** She is smarter than he is strong.
- **Correct:** She is smarter than he is stronger.

Examples of Parallel Structure in Sentences:

Incorrect Sentence	Corrected Version
I enjoy swimming, to read, and biking.	I enjoy swimming, reading, and biking.
He likes to run, hiking, and to swim.	He likes running, hiking, and swimming.
The job requires you to be organized, on time, and that you communicate clearly.	The job requires you to be organized, punctual, and communicative.

Tables and Charts for Quick Reference

Concept	Definition	Example
Simple Sentence	One independent clause	I finished my homework.
Compound Sentence	Two independent clauses joined by a conjunction	I finished my homework, and I played basketball.
Complex Sentence	One independent clause and one dependent clause	Because I finished my homework, I went to bed early.
Subject-Verb Agreement	Subject and verb must match in number	The dog runs. (singular); The dogs run. (plural)
Sentence Fragment	Incomplete sentence	Because I was late. (What happened?)
Run-on Sentence	Two clauses without punctuation or conjunction	I ran I jumped. (Should be: I ran, and I jumped.)
Parallel Structure	Same grammatical form in lists or comparisons	He likes running, swimming, and biking.

Practice Examples

Identify the sentence types.

Label each sentence as simple, compound, or complex.
1. I went to the park, and I played soccer.
2. After the rain stopped, we went outside.
3. She reads every day.
4. Because I was hungry, I made a sandwich and ate it.

Answers

1. Compound
2. Complex
3. Simple
4. Complex

TRIVIA CORNER

1: The shortest possible sentence in English is "Go."

2: The longest sentence ever written in literature is over 13,000 words long and appears in the novel Les Misérables.

3: James Joyce's Ulysses features a famous run-on sentence that goes on for over 4,000 words without any periods.

4: The word "and" is the most commonly used conjunction in English, but overuse can lead to run-on sentences.

5: Shakespeare often used sentence fragments and complex sentences for dramatic effect.

6: Parallel structure is common in famous speeches, like Martin Luther King Jr.'s "I Have a Dream."

7: Subject-verb agreement can be tricky in sentences where the subject comes after the verb.

8: The most common sentence structure in English is the simple sentence, but writers often mix it with compound and complex sentences.

9: The sentence "Buffalo buffalo Buffalo buffalo buffalo buffalo Buffalo buffalo" is grammatically correct!

10: Sentence fragments can be used intentionally in creative writing to convey emphasis or mood.

 ACTIVITY CORNER 3

Activity 1: Identifying Sentence Types

Identify whether the following sentences are simple, compound, or complex.

1. I finished my homework early.
2. Although I was tired, I stayed up late to study.
3. She wanted to go to the movie, but her friend was busy.
4. The dog barked loudly.
5. After the game, we went out for dinner.

Activity 2: Subject-Verb Agreement Fix

The following sentences contain subject-verb agreement errors. Identify and correct them.

1. The group of students are going to the library.
2. Every dog and cat like to sleep in the sun.
3. Neither the teacher nor the students was prepared for the surprise quiz.
4. The books on the shelf needs to be organized.
5. Either my brother or my parents is driving me to school today.

Activity 3: Sentence Fragment or Complete Sentence?

Instructions: Determine if each of the following is a sentence fragment or a complete sentence. If it's a fragment, rewrite it as a complete sentence.

1. After the concert ended.
2. She walked her dog to the park.
3. Because it was raining.
4. They went out for ice cream after the game.
5. Running down the street.

◎ ACTIVITY CORNER 3

Activity 4 : Correcting Run-on Sentences

Each of the following sentences is a run-on sentence. Rewrite each one to correct it, using periods, semicolons, or conjunctions.

1. She loves reading she goes to the library every week.
2. The sun is shining the weather is perfect for a picnic.
3. I studied all night I still didn't pass the test.
4. He cooked dinner it tasted amazing.
5. The car broke down we had to walk home.

Activity 5 : Parallel Structure Check

Identify whether each sentence uses parallel structure correctly. If not, rewrite the sentence with the correct parallel structure.

1. He likes swimming, to run, and biking.
2. The teacher told us to read the book, take notes, and reviewing for the test.
3. She enjoys dancing, singing, and playing the guitar.
4. The job requires attention to detail, creativity, and to be on time.
5. They were not only excited about the trip but also nervous about missing school.

4. Punctuation and Capitalization

Punctuation and Capitalization

Mastering punctuation and capitalization is essential for making your writing clear, professional, and engaging. Without proper punctuation, sentences can become confusing and the meaning can be lost. In this chapter, we will break down the essential rules of punctuation and capitalization and provide plenty of examples, tables, and activities to help you become a pro.

End Marks: Periods, Question Marks, and Exclamation Points

End marks help indicate when a thought or sentence is complete. Let's explore each one.

Periods (.)
- A period ends a declarative sentence or statement. It tells the reader, "This is the end of a thought."
  - Example: The cat is sleeping.
- Use periods for abbreviations as well:
  - Example: Dr. Smith is our school principal.

Question Marks (?)
- A question mark is used at the end of a direct question.
  - Example: What time does the movie start?
- Don't use multiple question marks:
  - Incorrect: Where are you going??
  - Correct: Where are you going?

Exclamation Points (!)
- Use an exclamation point for excitement, surprise, or strong emotion.
  - Example: That's amazing!
- However, overuse of exclamation points can make your writing less professional.
  - Avoid: This is so cool!!!

Common Errors with End Marks
- Mistake: Forgetting to add punctuation at the end of a sentence.
- Solution: Every complete sentence must end with either a period, question mark, or exclamation point.

Sentence	Correct End Mark
Are you coming to the party	Are you coming to the party?
I can't believe it	I can't believe it!
The dog ran into the yard	The dog ran into the yard.

Commas

Commas may be small, but they're one of the most commonly misused punctuation marks. They serve many purposes, from separating elements in a sentence to clarifying meaning.

Comma Usage:

1. In Lists
- Commas separate items in a list to make things clearer.
  - Example: I need to buy apples, oranges, bananas, and grapes.
- The comma before "and" is the Oxford comma. It's optional, but using it avoids confusion.
  - Example without Oxford comma: I need to buy apples, oranges, bananas and grapes.
  - Example with Oxford comma: I need to buy apples, oranges, bananas, and grapes.

2. In Compound Sentences
- When two independent clauses (complete thoughts) are joined by a conjunction (and, but, or, so), use a comma before the conjunction.
  - Example: I wanted to go to the park, but it started raining.

3. After Introductory Elements
- Use a comma after introductory phrases or words to set them apart from the main sentence.
  - Example: After dinner, we went for a walk.
  - Example: Unfortunately, I missed the bus.

4. With Nonessential Clauses

Commas set off nonessential (extra) information in a sentence.
- o Example: My brother, who lives in Chicago, is visiting next week.
- o If the information is essential to the sentence's meaning, don't use commas.
- o Example: Students who study hard get good grades.

Common Errors with Commas
- Comma Splice: Joining two independent clauses with just a comma.
  - o Incorrect: I went to the mall, I bought shoes.
  - o Correct: I went to the mall, and I bought shoes.

Usage	Example
Commas in Lists	She bought eggs, milk, bread, and butter.
Compound Sentences	He studied all night, but he still failed the test.
Introductory Elements	Before the game, we warmed up.
Nonessential Clauses	Mr. Lee, my math teacher, is very helpful.

Semicolons and Colons

Semicolons and colons are often misused, but when used correctly, they bring clarity and precision to your writing.

Semicolons (;)
- Semicolons connect related independent clauses without using a conjunction.
  - o Example: I have a lot of homework tonight; I can't go out.
- Semicolons can also separate items in a complex list where commas are already used within the items.
  - o Example: The guest list includes John, the chef; Maria, the artist; and Tim, the musician.

Colons (:)

- **Use a colon to introduce a list, explanation, or example.**
  - Example: You need to bring the following items: pencils, notebooks, and a calculator.
- **A colon can also be used to emphasize important information.**
  - Example: There was one thing he feared: failure.

Punctuation	Usage	Example
Semicolon	Connect related sentences without a conjunction	I have a meeting tomorrow; I need to get some rest.
Semicolon in Lists	Separate items that contain commas	We visited New York, New York; Paris, France; and Tokyo, Japan.
Colon	Introduce a list, example, or explanation	Bring the following items: snacks, water, and sunscreen.
Colon for Emphasis	Emphasize a point	The secret to her success is simple: hard work.

Quotation Marks and Dialogue

Quotation marks are essential for showing direct speech and distinguishing titles of short works.

Quoting Direct Speech

- Quotation marks enclose the exact words of a speaker.
  - Example: "I'm really tired," said Emma.

- When a quote follows a dialogue tag like said or asked, place a comma before the quote.
  - Example: He asked, "Are you coming to the game?"

Quoting Titles

- Use quotation marks for short works such as articles, short stories, poems, and songs.
  - Example: We read "The Tell-Tale Heart" in English class.

Formatting Dialogue

- Each time a different character speaks, start a new paragraph.
  - Example:
    - "Where are we going?" asked Sarah.
    - "To the park," replied Tom.

Rule	Example
Direct Speech	"I'm hungry," said Max.
Titles	We watched "The Simpsons" last night.
New Speaker, New Paragraph	"Can I come too?" asked John. "Sure," replied Susan.

Apostrophes

Apostrophes are used to show possession or to form contractions. Using them correctly helps avoid confusion.

Possessive Nouns

- Add **'s** to show ownership for singular nouns.
  - Example: The dog's leash (The leash belongs to the dog).

- For plural nouns that end in s, just add an apostrophe.
  - Example: The teachers' lounge (The lounge for multiple teachers).

Contractions

- Apostrophes replace missing letters in contractions.
  - Example: Don't = do not, I'm = I am

Common Errors with Apostrophes:
- Its vs. It's: It's is short for it is or it has, while its is possessive.
  - Example: It's raining outside. / The dog wagged its tail.

Incorrect	Correct
Its a nice day	It's a nice day
The cats tail	The cat's tail
Theyre excited	They're excited

Capitalization Rules

Capitalization highlights important words like proper nouns and the beginnings of sentences.

Proper Nouns

- Capitalize names of specific people, places, days of the week, and holidays.
  - Example: Sarah, New York, Monday, Christmas

- Sentence Beginnings: Always capitalize the first word of a sentence.
  - Example: The game was exciting.

Titles

- Capitalize the main words in titles, but leave out short words like and, of, the, unless they're the first word.

  - Example: The Great Gatsby

39

Common Capitalization Mistakes

- Failing to capitalize I or proper nouns.
- Over-capitalizing common nouns, such as the teacher instead of Ms. Smith

Punctuation and capitalization are essential for organizing your writing and making it easier to understand. By mastering these rules, you can ensure your writing is clear, professional, and error-free.

Correct the Punctuation and Capitalization

Below are the corrections and explanations for the sentences.

1) Original: where is your book asked the teacher
   - Corrected: "Where is your book?" asked the teacher.
   - Explanation:
     - The sentence is a question, so it needs a question mark.
     - Quotation marks are needed to show that these are the teacher's exact words.
     - Capitalization: The first word in the sentence ("Where") must be capitalized, and quotation marks must enclose the spoken words.

2) Original: i don't know if i'll be there or not
   - Corrected: I don't know if I'll be there or not.
   - Explanation:
     - Capitalization: The word "I" is always capitalized.
     - The apostrophe in "don't" shows it's a contraction of "do not."
     - The apostrophe in "I'll" shows it's a contraction of "I will."

3) Original: the teams uniforms were red and black
   - Corrected: The team's uniforms were red and black.
   - Explanation:
     - Capitalization: The first word of the sentence ("The") must be capitalized.
     - Apostrophe: "Team's" needs an apostrophe to show possession (the uniforms belong to the team). Without the apostrophe, "teams" would incorrectly be plural.

TRIVIA CORNER

1. **The Oxford Comma Debate:**
- *Fact:* The Oxford comma (also known as the serial comma) is a controversial topic among writers and editors. It's the comma placed before the final item in a list. While some style guides recommend using it for clarity, especially in complex lists, others argue it's unnecessary.
- *Example:* "I love my parents, Beyoncé, and Jay-Z" (with Oxford comma) vs. "I love my parents, Beyoncé and Jay-Z" (without Oxford comma).

2. **Capitalization in Roman Times:**
- *Fact:* The Romans wrote everything in uppercase, but their script differed from our modern alphabet. As we know them today, using uppercase and lowercase letters is a product of medieval European writing practices.

3. **The First Question Mark:**
- *Fact:* The first known use of a question mark dates back to the 8th century. It was initially shaped like a lightning bolt and used to mark a rhetorical question's end.

4. **Comma Misuse:**
- *Fact:* Commas can significantly alter the meaning of a sentence. For example, consider the difference between "Let's eat, Grandma!" and "Let's eat Grandma!"

5. **The Exclamation Point:**
- *Fact:* The exclamation point originally came from the Latin word "io," meaning "joy." It evolved into its modern form over time.

6. **Semicolons vs. Colons:**
- *Fact:* Semicolons and colons are often confused. A semicolon connects two closely related independent clauses, while a colon introduces a list or emphasizes information.

7. **Quotation Marks:**
- *Fact:* Quotation marks were first used in manuscripts to mark noteworthy passages. Today, they are essential for dialogue and citing sources.

8. **Apostrophe Misuse:**
- *Fact:* Apostrophes are one of the most misused punctuation marks. Many people mistakenly use "it's" when they mean "its." "It's" is a contraction of "it is," while "its" shows possession.

9. **The Evolution of Punctuation:**
- *Fact:* Punctuation wasn't always standard. In early manuscripts, scribes creatively used dots and marks to signify pauses or emphasis, eventually evolving into modern punctuation rules.

10. **The Longest Sentence:**
- *Fact:* The longest written sentence is in Victor Hugo's Les Misérables, stretching over 800 words. It contains multiple commas and semicolons to maintain grammatical correctness.

ACTIVITY CORNER 4
Activity: Punctuation and Capitalization

Activity 1: Fix the Punctuation

Correct the punctuation and capitalization in the following sentences.

1. where are you going tomorrow asked jessica
2. the students books were all over the floor
3. he didnt know whether to laugh cry or shout
4. can i borrow your pen for a minute
5. we will visit paris london and rome on our

Activity 2: Insert the Commas

Add commas where necessary.

1. My favorite colors are red blue green and yellow.
2. Before leaving make sure you have your keys.
3. The cake which was delicious was baked by my mom.
4. Sarah John and Emily went to the movies last night.
5. After the meeting we went out for coffee.

Activity 3: Semicolons and Colons Practice

Use semicolons or colons to correct the sentences below.

1. I have three things to buy eggs milk and bread.
2. It was raining heavily I decided to stay indoors.
3. The meeting starts at 9 00 please be on time.
4. She had one goal to win the race.
5. I love traveling I've been to Italy Spain and Greece.

 ACTIVITY CORNER 4

Activity: Vocabulary Games and Challenges

Activity 4 Quotation Marks in Dialogue :

Insert the correct quotation marks and punctuation in the following sentences.

1. jessica said i can't wait for summer break
2. can you believe he just said i'm not going to the party
3. the teacher told us finish your homework tonight
4. is the answer really true she asked
5. i read the short story the lottery for class

Activity 5: Apostrophe Usage

Correct the apostrophe mistakes in the following sentences.

1. The cats toys were scattered all over the house.
2. Its raining outside, so don't forget your umbrella.
3. The girls locker room is on the left.
4. The childrens books were organized by genre.
5. I can't believe its already time for the exam.

5. Pronouns and Their Correct Usage

Pronouns and Their Correct Usage

Pronouns are crucial in grammar as they help to avoid repetition by replacing nouns. Using pronouns correctly is important for making sentences clearer and more concise. In this chapter, we will cover the various types of pronouns, how to match them with their antecedents, avoid vague pronouns, and use the correct pronoun case in different sentence structures.

Types of Pronouns :

Pronouns fall into various categories, each serving a unique purpose in writing and speaking. Let's explore the most common types:

Type of Pronoun	Definition	Examples
Personal Pronouns	Refer to specific people or things	I, you, he, she, it, we, they (subject) me, him, her, us, them (object)
Relative Pronouns	Introduce relative clauses to give more information	who, whom, whose, which, that
Reflexive Pronouns	Refer back to the subject in the sentence	myself, yourself, himself, herself, itself, ourselves, themselves
Indefinite Pronouns	Refer to nonspecific people or things	anyone, everyone, somebody, nobody, anything, all
Demonstrative Pronouns	Point to specific things or people	this, that, these, those

Examples in Sentences:

Personal Pronouns:

- She is working on her homework.
- They invited me to the event.

Relative Pronouns:

- This is the book that I was looking for.
- The student who won the award is in my class.

Reflexive Pronouns:

- I did it myself.
- They helped themselves to the food.

Indefinite Pronouns:

- Everyone needs to arrive on time.
- Nobody knew the answer to the question.

Demonstrative Pronouns:

- This is my favorite book.
- Those are my shoes.

Table: Types of Pronouns in Sentences

Type	Sentence Example
Personal Pronouns	He loves to read.
Relative Pronouns	The girl who won the race is my friend.
Reflexive Pronouns	She looked at herself in the mirror.
Indefinite Pronouns	Someone left their bag.
Demonstrative Pronouns	These are the answers you need.

Pronoun-Antecedent Agreement :

The antecedent is the noun to which the pronoun refers. Pronouns must agree with their antecedents in number (singular or plural) and gender (masculine, feminine, or neutral). Lack of agreement can lead to unclear sentences..

Antecedent	Pronoun
The girl is studying.	She is studying.
The dogs are barking.	They are barking.
John forgot his book.	He forgot his book.

Examples of Agreement:

Singular Antecedent, Singular Pronoun:
- The student lost her notebook.
- The car broke down, so it was towed.

Plural Antecedent, Plural Pronoun:
- The children finished their homework.
- The teachers shared their resources.

Common Mistakes:
- Incorrect: Each student should bring their book.
- Correct: Each student should bring his or her book. (Since "each" is singular, use "his or her.")

Table: Pronoun-Antecedent Agreement

Antecedent	Pronoun	Correct Example
The boy	He	He is my friend.
The boys	They	They are playing soccer.
The teacher	She	She explained the lesson.
The teachers	They	They met after school.

Avoiding Vague Pronoun References

A vague pronoun reference occurs when it's unclear what noun the pronoun refers to, confusing. To avoid this, make sure that the antecedent is clear.

Vague Reference Example:
- Unclear: When John and Mark arrived, he was excited.
- (Who was excited? John or Mark?)

Clear Reference Example:
- Clear: When John and Mark arrived, John was excited.

More Examples:
1. Vague: If the students don't study, they will fail.
2. Clear: If the students don't study, the students will fail.
3. Vague: The teacher told Sarah that she needs more practice.
4. Clear: The teacher told Sarah that Sarah needs more practice.

Table: Correcting Vague Pronouns

Vague Sentence	Correct Sentence
When John and Peter entered, he looked happy.	When John and Peter entered, John looked happy.
The book was on the table, but it was torn.	The book was on the table, but the book was torn.

Pronoun Case: Subjective, Objective, and Possessive

Pronouns have different forms based on their function in a sentence. They can be subjective (used as the subject), objective (used as the object), or possessive (show ownership).

Pronoun Case	Pronouns	Example
Subjective	I, you, he, she, it, we, they	She is going to the store.
Objective	me, you, him, her, it, us, them	The teacher gave him the assignment.
Possessive	my, your, his, her, its, our, their	That is my book.

Examples:

Subjective Pronoun:
- o She won the race.
- o They are playing soccer.

Objective Pronoun:
- o The teacher helped me.
- o I gave the ball to him.

Possessive Pronoun:
- o This is my backpack.
- o The house is theirs.

Table: Pronoun Case in Use

Function	Subjective Pronouns	Objective Pronouns	Possessive Pronouns
Subject of the sentence	I, you, he, she, they	N/A	N/A
Object of the sentence	N/A	me, you, him, her, them	N/A
Ownership	N/A	N/A	my, your, his, her, their

Common Pronoun Errors and Fixes

Error 1: Incorrect Pronoun Case
- Incorrect: Me and Tom went to the park.
- Correct: Tom and I went to the park.

Error 2: Using the Wrong Possessive
- Incorrect: The cat lost it's collar.
- Correct: The cat lost its collar. (It's = "it is"; its = possessive)

Error 3: Vague Pronoun Reference
- Incorrect: When the car hit the pole, it broke.
- Correct: When the car hit the pole, the pole broke. (Clarifies what "it" refers)

Error 4: Pronoun-Antecedent Agreement
- Incorrect: Neither of the girls brought their lunch.
- Correct: Neither of the girls brought her lunch. ("Neither" is singular, so the pronoun should also be singular.)

Error 5: Shifting Pronoun Point of View
- Incorrect: When you study hard, one can get better grades.
- Correct: When you study hard, you can get better grades. (Maintain a consistent point of view. Switching between "you" and "one" creates confusion.)

Error 6: Incorrect Reflexive Pronoun Usage
- Incorrect: Sarah and myself will present the project.
- Correct: Sarah and I will present the project. (Reflexive pronouns like "myself" should only be used when the subject and object are the same person: "I hurt myself.")

TRIVIA CORNER

- The word "pronoun" comes from Latin: pro means "for" or "in place of," and nomen means "name." So, a pronoun is literally a "substitute for a noun."
- The longest personal pronoun in the English language is ourselves — an 8-letter reflexive pronoun!
- In Old English, there was a separate pronoun for "you two" called git. This dual pronoun was used when talking to exactly two people.
- The singular "they" was officially accepted by the Merriam-Webster Dictionary in 2019 as a gender-neutral pronoun, although it has been used in this way since the 1300s.
- The pronoun "who" has been used in English for over 1,000 years, making it one of the oldest words.
- In some languages, like Japanese, pronouns are often left out altogether because the context clearly identifies who or what is being referred to!
- The most commonly used pronoun in English is "it," which refers to anything that isn't a person or when the subject is unknown or unimportant.
- English doesn't have a formal second-person pronoun (like "vous" in French), but "thou" used to be the formal second-person singular pronoun until it fell out of favor in the 1600s.
- The reflexive pronoun "myself" is one of the most commonly misused pronouns in English, especially when people say things like "John and myself" instead of "John and I."
- The pronoun "I" is always capitalized in English, which is unusual because most other languages, like Spanish and French, don't capitalize their first-person pronouns.

◎ ACTIVITY CORNER 5

ACTIVITY 1: PRONOUN IDENTIFICATION QUIZ

Objective: Identify the types of pronouns in sentences.

Instructions: Below are five sentences. Identify the type of pronoun in each bolded word (personal, relative, reflexive, demonstrative, indefinite).

1. **She** gave the book to him.
2. **This** is my favorite book.
3. The players **who** won the game were very excited.
4. **They** finished their homework before the bell rang.
5. **Nobody** answered the question.

ACTIVITY 2 : CORRECT THE VAGUE PRONOUN REFERENCE

Objective: Rewrite the sentence to eliminate vague pronouns.

Instructions: The following sentences contain vague pronouns. Rewrite each sentence to clarify the pronoun's reference.

1. When Alex spoke to Chris, he was confused.
2. Sarah gave the book to Emily, and she put it on the shelf.
3. After the teacher handed the paper to James, he lost it.
4. When John helped Michael, he thanked him.
5. The dog chased the cat, and it ran into the yard.

ACTIVITY 3 : PRONOUN-ANTECEDENT AGREEMENT MATCHING

Objective: Match the correct pronoun with its antecedent in each sentence.

Instructions: Match the pronouns in Column A with their correct antecedents from Column B.

Column A (Pronouns)	Column B (Antecedents)
1. His	A. The students
2. Their	B. Emily
3. Her	C. The dog
4. Its	D. The boys

ACTIVITY 4 : PRONOUN CASE QUIZ

Objective: Choose the correct pronoun case for each sentence.

Instructions: Select the correct pronoun (subjective, objective, possessive) to complete each sentence.

1. The teacher gave the assignment to (me/I).
2. She and (him/he) went to the library.
3. This is (my/mine) book.
4. Between you and (me/I), this is a secret.
5. (We/Us) students studied for the test.

ACTIVITY 5 : FILL IN THE BLANKS WITH THE CORRECT PRONOUN

Objective: Complete each sentence by choosing the correct pronoun from the list provided.

Instructions: Choose the correct pronoun from the options to fill in the blanks.

1. Neither of the girls brought _____ lunch. (her, their)
2. The teachers, along with the principal, discussed _____ plans. (his, their)
3. Each student should bring _____ notebook to class. (his or her, their)
4. Both of the players did _____ best in the game. (his, their)
5. Anyone can bring _____ ideas to the meeting. (their, his or her)

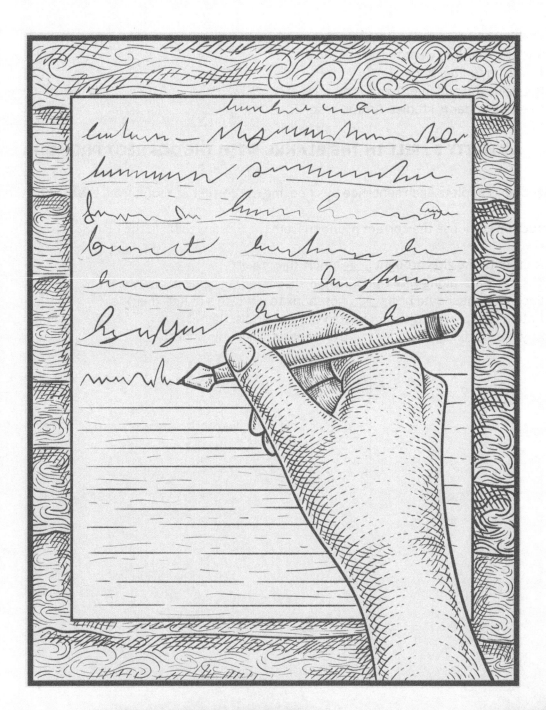

Verb Tenses and Consistency :

Verb tenses are crucial for conveying the timing of an action. This chapter aims to help you grasp the various verb tenses, maintain consistency in your writing, and effectively use active and passive voice. You will also learn how to deal with irregular verbs.

Overview of Tenses

Tenses indicate the time of an action or a state of being. Three main tenses—present, past, and future—each can be combined with Simple, perfect, and progressive aspects.

Simple Tenses

Present Tense

The present tense is used to describe actions happening now or habitual actions.
- **Simple Present**: Describes habitual actions or general truths.

  - Example: "I walk to school every day."

Past Tense

The past tense describes actions that occurred in the past and are no longer happening.
- **Simple Past**: Describes actions that started and finished in the past.

  - Example: "I walked to school yesterday."

Future Tense

The future tense describes actions that will happen in the future.
- **Simple Future**: Describes actions that will occur.

  - Example: "I will walk to school tomorrow."

Perfect Tenses

The perfect tense describes actions completed by a certain point in time.

- **Present Perfect:** Describes an action that started in the past and continues into the present or has been completed.

  - **Example:** "I have walked to school for five years."

- **Past Perfect:** Describes an action that was completed before another action in the past.

  - **Example:** "I had walked to school before it started raining."

- **Future Perfect:** Describes an action that will be completed before a certain point in the future.

  - **Example:** "By tomorrow, I will have walked to school for a full week."

Progressive Tenses

The progressive tense describes ongoing actions.

- **Present Progressive:** Describes an action happening right now.

  - Example: "I am walking to school."

- **Past Progressive**: Describes an action that was happening in the past when another action occurred.

  - Example: "I was walking to school when it started raining."

- **Future Progressive:** Describes an action that will be happening at a specific point in the future.

  - Example: "I will be walking to school when you arrive."

Table of Simple, Perfect and Progressive Tense

Tense	Simple	Perfect	Progressive
Present	I walk	I have walked	I am walking
Past	I walked	I had walked	I was walking
Future	I will walk	I will have walked	I will be walking

Shifts in Tenses

Maintaining consistent verb tense is essential to clear writing. Shifting between tenses can confuse the reader. Let's look at a common error:

Incorrect Tense Shift:
- "I walked to school, and now I am eating lunch."
- (The shift from past "walked" to present "am eating" is jarring.)

Corrected Tense Consistency:
- "I walked to school, and then I ate lunch."
- (Both actions are in the past, maintaining consistency.)

Tips for Avoiding Tense Shifts:
- Use the same tense when describing actions that happen in the same time frame.
- Be mindful of time indicators like "yesterday," "tomorrow," or "now" to keep tenses consistent.

Active vs. Passive Voice

The active voice emphasizes the doer of the action, while the passive voice emphasizes the receiver of the action. The active voice is generally clearer and more direct, making it a preferred choice for strong writing.

Active Voice:
- Example: "The teacher graded the tests."
  - (The subject, "the teacher," is doing the action.)

Passive Voice:
- Example: "The tests were graded by the teacher."
  - (The subject, "the tests," receives the action.)

Table: Active Passive Voice

Active Voice	Passive Voice
1. The teacher explained the lesson.	The lesson was explained by the teacher.
2. They will complete the project tomorrow.	The project will be completed by them tomorrow.
3. The chef cooked the meal.	The meal was cooked by the chef.
4. She is writing a letter.	A letter is being written by her.
5. The team won the game.	The game was won by the team.
6. The company designs new software.	New software is designed by the company.
7. He had cleaned the house.	The house had been cleaned by him.
8. The students are reading the book.	The book is being read by the students.
9. They will announce the results soon.	The results will be announced soon by them.
10. She presented the report.	The report was presented by her.

Irregular Verbs

Irregular verbs don't follow the typical -ed ending rule in the past tense. These verbs have unique forms that need to be memorized.

Common Irregular Verbs:

Base Form	Past Form	Past Participle
Go	Went	Gone
Run	Ran	Run
Speak	Spoke	Spoken
Write	Wrote	Written
Take	Took	Taken

Base Form	Past Tense	Past Participle
Begin	Began	Begun
Break	Broke	Broken
Choose	Chose	Chosen
Come	Came	Come
Do	Did	Done
Drink	Drank	Drunk
Drive	Drove	Driven
Eat	Ate	Eaten
Fly	Flew	Flown
Forget	Forgot	Forgotten
Give	Gave	Given
Go	Went	Gone
See	Saw	Seen
Take	Took	Taken
Write	Wrote	Written

Trivia Corner

- *12 tenses: While there are indeed 12 tenses in English, it's important to note that some of these tenses are less commonly used in everyday conversation.*

- *"Be" verb: The statement is correct that "be" is irregular, but it could also be mentioned that it's one of the most frequently used verbs in English.*

- *Present perfect vs. simple past: The distinction between the present perfect and simple past in British and American English is accurate, but it's worth noting that there are also regional variations within both countries.*

- *Passive voice: The statement is correct that passive voice is more common in scientific and technical writing, but it's also used in other contexts, such as legal or bureaucratic documents.*

- *Irregular verbs: The statement is correct that irregular verbs are often the most common verbs, but it could also be mentioned that there are many regular verbs that are also frequently used.*

- *Latin and Greek influence: The statement is correct that Latin and Greek have influenced many irregular verbs, but it could also be mentioned that many other languages have influenced English vocabulary and grammar.*

- *Disappearing verb forms: The statement is correct that some verb forms are disappearing, but it's worth noting that language is constantly evolving, and new verb forms may also be emerging.*

- *"Shall" vs. "Will": The statement is correct that "will" has largely replaced "shall" in modern English, but it's worth noting that "shall" is still used in some formal or literary contexts.*

- *Progressive tenses: The statement is correct that progressive tenses are less common in other languages, but it's worth noting that there are some languages that have similar constructions.*

- *Passive voice: The statement is correct that overusing passive voice can make writing sound awkward, but it's important to note that there are times when passive voice is appropriate and effective.*

# ◎ ACTIVITY CORNER 6

Activity 1: Identify the Verb Tense

Read each sentence below and identify the verb tense used. Choose from the following:

simple present, simple past, simple future, present perfect, past perfect, future perfect, present progressive, past progressive, or future progressive.

1. She has already finished her homework.
2. We will be traveling to New York next week.
3. They were eating dinner when the phone rang.
4. I study every day for an hour.
5. By the time she arrives, I will have left.

Activity 2: Correct the Tense Shift

The sentences below have incorrect shifts in tense. Rewrite them to maintain consistent verb tenses.

1. She walked into the room and sees her friend.
2. I was watching TV when my phone rings.
3. They will visit us last week and had a great time.
4. He eats dinner and then washed the dishes.
5. The dog barked loudly as the mailman approaches.

Activity 3 : Active vs. Passive Voice

Rewrite the following passive sentences in the active voice.

1. The ball was kicked by John.
2. The homework was completed by the students.
3. The cake was baked by Sarah.
4. The letter was written by the teacher.
5. The project was finished by the team.

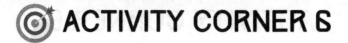

Activity 4 : Fill in the Irregular Verb

Complete the sentences below with the correct form of the irregular verb :

1. Yesterday, I _____ (go) to the store.
2. She has _____ (eat) lunch already.
3. We _____ (see) the movie last night.
4. He has _____ (do) his homework.
5. They _____ (run) in the race yesterday.

Activity 5 : Match the Tense to the Sentence

Match the verb tense to the sentence by drawing a line to the correct tense.

1. I have lived here for ten years.
2. She was walking to school when it started raining.
3. They will travel to Paris next year.
4. He had already left when they arrived.
5. We are studying for the test right now.

Tenses:

1. Future simple
2. Present perfect
3. Past progressive
4. Present progressive
5. Past perfect

7. Modifiers and Their Placement

Introduction :

Modifiers play an essential role in improving the clarity and quality of your writing. They are words or phrases that provide more information about another word in the sentence, usually a noun or verb. In this chapter, we will explore how to use modifiers such as adjectives and adverbs effectively, avoid common mistakes like misplaced or dangling modifiers, and learn how to correctly use comparatives and superlatives.

Adjectives and Adverbs as Modifiers

Modifiers help enhance sentences by adding details that make the writing more descriptive. Adjectives modify (describe) nouns, while adverbs modify verbs, adjectives, or other adverbs.

Using Modifiers to Enhance Sentences

Let's take a look at how adjectives and adverbs can bring a sentence to life:

Example 1 (Adjectives):

- Without adjectives: The girl smiled.
- With adjectives: The happy, young girl smiled brightly.

Here, "happy" and "young" describe the girl.

Example 2 (Adverbs):

- Without adverbs: He ran.
- With adverbs: He ran quickly to catch the bus.

In this example, "quickly" is an adverb that modifies the verb "ran."

Practical Tip:

Modifiers are helpful, but too many can clutter your sentence. It's important to use them carefully and avoid overloading your sentences with too many unnecessary details.

While the sentence is packed with modifiers, it's harder to read. Here's how we can simplify it:

- **Simplified sentence**: The talented player kicked the ball powerfully.

Table: Common Adjectives and Adverbs

Adjectives	Adverbs
Beautiful	Beautifully
Bright	Brightly
Strong	Strongly
Careful	Carefully
Quiet	Quietly
Quick	Quickly

Exercise 1: Adding Modifiers

Add appropriate adjectives or adverbs to the following sentences:

1. The _____ car sped down the road.
2. She _____ opened the door.
3. The _____ dog barked _____ at the strangers.

Answers: (Note: Multiple correct answers can depend on the modifiers chosen. Here are a few examples.)

1. The red car sped down the road.
2. She quickly opened the door.
3. The big dog barked loudly at the strangers.

Feel free to mix and match adjectives and adverbs depending on the tone or context you're aiming for!

Misplaced and Dangling Modifiers

Modifiers must be carefully placed in sentences to describe the word they modify clearly; when misplaced, they can confuse the reader or alter the sentence's meaning.

Misplaced Modifiers

A misplaced modifier is when a word or phrase is not close enough to the word it describes, making the sentence unclear or awkward.

Example 1:

- **Incorrect:** The man walked his dog wearing a hat.

This makes it sound like the dog was wearing the hat! The modifier "wearing a hat" is misplaced.

- **Correct**: The man, wearing a hat, walked his dog.

Now, it's clear that the man is wearing the hat.

Example 2:

- **Incorrect:** She spent nearly $100 on clothes.

This sentence means she almost spent $100 but didn't. However, if we meant that she spent a little less than $100, we must adjust the modifier.

- **Correct**: She spent nearly $100 on clothes.

Table: Fixing Misplaced Modifiers

Incorrect	Correct
The students watched the movie eating popcorn.	Eating popcorn, the students watched the movie.
I heard that he was leaving from a friend.	I heard from a friend that he was leaving.
She served the cake to the guests on paper plates.	She served the cake on paper plates to the guests.

Dangling Modifiers

A dangling modifier occurs when the modifier doesn't relate to any word in the sentence.

Example 1:
- **Incorrect**: After finishing the homework, the TV was turned on.

Who finished the homework? The subject isn't clear.
- **Correct**: After finishing the homework, I turned on the TV.

Now, we know it was "I" who finished the homework.

Example 2:
- **Incorrect**: Running down the street, the trees blew in the wind.

This sentence makes it sound like the trees were running!
- **Correct**: Running down the street, I saw the trees blowing in the wind.

Exercise 2: **Fixing Misplaced and Dangling Modifiers**
Rewrite the following sentences to correct the misplaced or dangling modifiers:
1. Walking to school, the rain started to fall.
2. She handed the homework to the teacher in a hurry.
3. The boy ate his sandwich sitting on the bench.

Comparatives and Superlatives

When comparing two things, we use comparatives by adding "-er" to short adjectives or "more" to longer adjectives.

Example 1:
- Lisa is taller than Jane.

Here, we use "taller" because we're comparing two people.

Superlatives
When comparing three or more things, we use superlatives by adding "-est" to short adjectives or "most" to longer adjectives.

Example 2:
- Lisa is the tallest person in the class.

Now, we're comparing Lisa to a larger group of people, so we use the superlative "tallest."

Table: Comparatives and Superlatives

Adjective	Comparative	Superlative
Tall	Taller	Tallest
Happy	Happier	Happiest
Difficult	More difficult	Most difficult
Fast	Faster	Fastest
Beautiful	More beautiful	Most beautiful

Common Errors with Comparatives and Superlatives

- **Incorrect**: She is more taller than her sister.
    - **Correct**: She is taller than her sister.

- **Incorrect**: Of the two players, John is the fastest.
    - **Correct**: Of the two players, John is faster.

Modifiers are essential tools in writing that make sentences more descriptive and interesting. In this chapter, you've learned how to use adjectives and adverbs, avoid misplaced and dangling modifiers, and correctly use comparative and superlative forms. By practicing these concepts, you can enhance your writing and avoid common mistakes that make sentences unclear.

Trivia Corner

- *Double Duty: Some words can function as adjectives and adverbs, depending on their use. For instance, "fast" can describe a "fast car" (adjective) or a "fast runner" (adverb).*

- *Longest Single-Word Modifier: The longest single-word modifier in English is antidisestablishmentarianism, which describes opposition to withdrawing state support for an established church.*

- *Comparative and Superlative Forms: The comparative and superlative forms of "bad" are "worse" and "worst," respectively. While "badder" might be used in informal speech, it's generally considered incorrect in formal writing.*

- *Misplaced Modifiers: A misplaced modifier can lead to humorous misunderstandings. For example, "I saw a dog on my way to school" could imply that the dog is attending school.*

- *Shakespeare's Superlatives: Shakespeare often used double superlatives like "most unkindest" in his plays, a practice that's considered redundant in modern English.*

- *Silent Modifiers: Sometimes, adjectives are implied even when they aren't explicitly stated. In the phrase "He ran fast," for example, "fast" modifies "ran," even though they aren't directly adjacent.*

- *Irregular Comparative and Superlative Forms: Some adjectives have irregular comparative and superlative forms. For instance, "good" becomes "better" and "best," and "bad" becomes "worse" and "worst."*

- *Dangling Modifiers: A dangling modifier can create confusion. For example, "After reading the book, the movie was disappointing" implies that the movie read the book.*

- *Adverb Endings: Most adverbs end in "-ly," but there are exceptions like "well" and "fast."*

- *Longest Adjective: The longest adjective in English is pneumonoultramicroscopicsilicovolcanoconiosis, a term used to describe a lung disease caused by inhaling very fine silicate or quartz dust.*

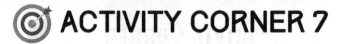

◎ ACTIVITY CORNER 7

ACTIVITY 1: IDENTIFY THE MODIFIER

Read each sentence below and underline the modifier. Then, could you specify whether the modifier is an adjective or an adverb.

1. The energetic puppy played happily in the yard.
2. She quickly finished her homework before dinner.
3. The old tree swayed gently in the wind.
4. The large, colorful balloon floated away.
5. He drove carefully on the icy roads.

ACTIVITY 2: FIX THE MISPLACED MODIFIERS

Rewrite the following sentences to correct the misplaced modifiers:

1. The teacher handed out tests to the students with a smile.
2. She saw a bird looking out the window with a bright red beak.
3. Covered in cheese, I ordered the pizza.
4. The kids walked home carrying their backpacks singing loudly.
5. He nearly ate all the ice cream in the fridge.

ACTIVITY 3: CORRECT THE DANGLING MODIFIERS

Rewrite the sentences to correct the dangling modifiers:

1. After eating lunch, the dishes were cleaned.
2. Driving home, the weather turned stormy.
3. Looking out of the window, the view was breathtaking.
4. Walking down the street, the trees seemed to be dancing.
5. By working hard, success was achieved.

ACTIVITY 4: COMPARATIVES AND SUPERLATIVES

Complete the sentences by using the correct form (comparative or superlative) of the adjectives in parentheses:

1. John is _____ (tall) than Mark, but Sam is the _____ (tall) in the class.
2. This book is _____ (interesting) than the one I read last week.
3. Of all my friends, Sarah is the _____ (funny).
4. Today's weather is _____ (bad) than yesterday.
5. Out of all the players, Leo is the _____ (good).

ACTIVITY 5: ADJECTIVES OR ADVERBS?

Choose the correct word to complete the sentence in the following sentences: adjective or adverb.

1. The dog barked (loud/loudly) during the night.
2. The (happy/happily) child skipped down the street.
3. She sang the song (beautiful/beautifully) at the talent show.
4. We stayed at a (nice/nicely) hotel during our vacation.
5. He drove (careful/carefully) to avoid the potholes.

8. Clauses and Phrases

Clauses and phrases are the building blocks of sentence structure. Understanding how they work is essential for writing clear, effective sentences. This chapter will explore independent and dependent clauses, subordinate and relative clauses, and how to enhance your writing with appositive and prepositional phrases.

Independent and Dependent Clauses

What is a Clause?

A clause is a group of words with a subject and a verb. Clauses can be independent (able to stand alone as a sentence) or dependent (relying on another clause to make sense).

Independent Clauses

An independent clause expresses a complete thought and can function as a full sentence.

- Example 1: She studied for her exam.
- Example 2: The cat is sleeping.

Dependent Clauses

A dependent clause adds extra information but cannot stand alone. It usually starts with a subordinating conjunction like because, when, if, or although.

- Example 1: When she studied for her exam. (Incomplete thought—what happened after she studied?)
- Example 2: Because the cat is sleeping. (Incomplete thought—what is happening while the cat sleeps?)

Combining Independent and Dependent Clauses

Combining independent and dependent clauses creates complex sentences that convey more detailed information.

73

- **Example 1**: When she studied for her exam, she felt prepared. (Dependent clause: When she studied for her exam + Independent clause: she felt prepared.)

- **Example 2**: I'll keep the volume low because the cat is sleeping. (Dependent clause: Because the cat is sleeping + Independent clause: I'll keep the volume low.)

Table: Identifying Independent and Dependent Clauses

Sentence	Independent Clause	Dependent Clause
The teacher was happy because the students passed the test.	The teacher was happy	because the students passed
If the weather improves, we will go hiking.	we will go hiking	If the weather improves
Although it was raining, they continued the game.	they continued the game	Although it was raining
She stayed up late so she could finish her project.	She stayed up late	so she could finish her project

More Examples of Subordinating Conjunctions

Purpose	Subordinating Conjunctions	Example Sentence
Cause/Reason	because, since, as	Since it was raining, we stayed indoors.
Time	when, after, before, as soon as	When the movie ended, we went out for ice cream.
Condition	if, unless, provided that	Unless you study, you won't pass the test.
Contrast	although, even though, though	Although she was tired, she finished her homework.
Purpose	so that, in order that	He studied hard so that he could get a scholarship.
Result	so, such that	She was so excited that she couldn't sleep.

Subordinate and Relative Clauses

Subordinate Clauses

A subordinate clause is a dependent clause that provides additional information and typically starts with a subordinating conjunction.

- Example 1: If you study hard, you will do well.
  - Subordinate clause: If you study hard
- Example 2: Although it was difficult, they finished the project.
  - Subordinate clause: Although it was difficult

Relative Clauses

A relative clause is a subordinate clause that gives extra information about a noun. It usually starts with a relative pronoun such as who, whom, whose, which, or that.

- Example 1: The athlete who won the race received a medal.
  - Relative clause: who won the race (describes "the athlete")
- Example 2: The book that I borrowed was exciting.
  - Relative clause: that I borrowed (describes "the book")

Table: Subordinate and Relative Clauses

Sentence	Type of Clause	Explanation
Although she was late, she finished the test on time.	Subordinate Clause	Although she was late explains the condition.
The cake that she baked was delicious.	Relative Clause	that she baked gives more information about "the cake."
If we win the game, we'll go out for pizza.	Subordinate Clause	If we win the game explains the condition.
The students who studied the hardest got the best grades.	Relative Clause	who studied the hardest describes "the students."

Relative Pronouns and Their Functions

Relative Pronoun	Example Sentence	Use
who	The teacher who helped me was kind.	Refers to people
whom	The friend whom I trust is moving away.	Refers to people (object form)
whose	The artist whose work you admire is here.	Shows possession
which	The dog which barked all night is sleeping now.	Refers to animals or things
that	The book that I read was amazing.	Refers to people, animals, or things

Table: Common Subordinating Conjunctions and Their Use in Subordinate Clauses

Subordinating Conjunction	Purpose	Example Sentence
after	Time	After the movie ended, we went out for dinner.
because	Reason/Cause	She left early because she had an appointment.
unless	Condition	Unless it rains, we'll have the picnic outside.
although	Contrast	Although it was difficult, she managed to solve the problem.

Appositive and Prepositional Phrases

An appositive phrase is a noun or noun phrase that renames or clarifies another noun in the sentence. It is often set off by commas if it adds non-essential information.

- Example 1: My best friend, a talented artist, won the contest.
  - A talented artist gives extra information about my best friend.

- Example 2: The red convertible car sped down the highway.
  - A red convertible adds more detail about the car.

Essential vs. Non-Essential Appositives

- Essential Appositive: My brother Tom is coming home tomorrow. (Here, Tom must clarify which brother is being talked about.)
- Non-Essential Appositive: Tom, my brother, is coming home tomorrow. (Here, my brother is non-essential since we already know who Tom is.)

Prepositional Phrases

A prepositional phrase consists of a preposition and its object. It adds information about location, time, or direction.

- Example 1: She sat by the window.
  - By the window tells where she sat.
- Example 2: The meeting will start at 3:00 PM.
  - At 3:00 PM tells when the meeting will start.

Table: Common Prepositional Phrases and Their Uses

Prepositional Phrase	Type of Information	Example Sentence
by the river	Location	We had a picnic by the river.
at midnight	Time	The party ended at midnight.
with a smile	Manner	She greeted me with a smile.
between the trees	Location	We walked between the trees.
during the summer	Time	I went to camp during the summer.

- Example 1: My best friend, a talented artist, won the contest.
  - A talented artist gives extra information about my best friend.

- Example 2: The red convertible car sped down the highway.
  - A red convertible adds more detail about the car.

Essential vs. Non-Essential Appositives

- Essential Appositive: My brother Tom is coming home tomorrow. (Here, Tom must clarify which brother is being talked about.)
- Non-Essential Appositive: Tom, my brother, is coming home tomorrow. (Here, my brother is non-essential since we already know who Tom is.)

Prepositional Phrases

A prepositional phrase consists of a preposition and its object. It adds information about location, time, or direction.

- Example 1: She sat by the window.
  - By the window tells where she sat.
- Example 2: The meeting will start at 3:00 PM.
  - At 3:00 PM tells when the meeting will start.

Table: Common Prepositional Phrases and Their Uses

Prepositional Phrase	Type of Information	Example Sentence
by the river	Location	We had a picnic by the river.
at midnight	Time	The party ended at midnight.
with a smile	Manner	She greeted me with a smile.
between the trees	Location	We walked between the trees.
during the summer	Time	I went to camp during the summer.

More Practical Examples

Let's take a more practical approach by looking at how different types of clauses and phrases enhance the meaning of sentences:

Example 1: Independent and Dependent Clauses
- Sentence: I missed the bus and had to walk to school.
  - Because I missed the bus (dependent clause) + I had to walk to school (independent clause)

Example 2: Subordinate and Relative Clauses
- Sentence: The teacher, who has been teaching for 20 years, gave us great advice.
  - Who has been teaching for 20 years (relative clause, describing the teacher)

Example 3: Appositive Phrases
- Sentence: My brother, a skilled chef, cooked us dinner last night.
  - A skilled chef (appositive phrase, describing my brother)

Common Mistakes in Clauses and Phrases, with Solutions and Tricks

Mistake	Explanation	Solution	Trick to Remember
Fragmented Sentence: Only using a dependent clause without an independent clause.	A dependent clause cannot stand alone because it doesn't form a complete thought.	Add an independent clause to complete the sentence.	Ask yourself: Can this sentence stand alone? If not, it needs more information. Example: Although I was tired. → Although I was tired, I finished my homework.
Comma Splice: Joining two independent clauses with only a comma.	Two independent clauses cannot be linked by just a comma.	Use a coordinating conjunction (like and, but, or) or a semicolon.	Remember FANBOYS (For, And, Nor, But, Or, Yet, So) for coordinating conjunctions. Example: She studied, she passed. → She studied, and she passed.
Misplacing the Appositive: Misplacing the appositive phrase so it doesn't clearly refer to the noun it's supposed to describe.	The appositive should be next to the noun it is renaming or describing.	Move the appositive next to the noun it describes.	Keep the appositive right after the noun it modifies. Example: A skilled chef, my brother made dinner.

Mistake	Explanation	Solution	Trick to Remember
Dangling Modifier: A phrase or clause that doesn't clearly refer to any word in the sentence.	The modifier is not clearly attached to the noun or subject it is supposed to describe.	Rewrite the sentence so that the modifier clearly describes the subject.	Make sure the subject of the sentence follows the phrase. Example: Running down the street, the car almost hit me. → Running down the street, I almost got hit by the car.
Unnecessary Relative Clauses: Using a relative clause that doesn't add new or useful information.	A relative clause should add important details, not repeat information.	Remove or replace the redundant relative clause.	If the relative clause is repetitive, remove it. Example: The teacher, who is a teacher, gave us homework. → The teacher gave us homework.
Missing or Misplaced Prepositional Phrase: The prepositional phrase is either missing or placed in a confusing part of the sentence.	Prepositional phrases provide clarity, and their placement affects the meaning of the sentence.	Ensure prepositional phrases are placed correctly and don't disrupt the flow.	Place the prepositional phrase near the word it modifies. Example: She saw the man with binoculars. (confusing) → She saw the man through binoculars.
Run-on Sentence: Combining multiple independent clauses without proper punctuation.	A run-on sentence occurs when two or more independent clauses are joined without the proper punctuation or conjunction.	Break the sentence into smaller sentences or use the correct punctuation.	If you have more than one independent clause, break it up! Example: She studied she passed the test. → She studied. She passed the test.

Tips and Tricks for Avoiding Mistakes:

1. **Dependent Clause Test**: Can the clause stand alone? If not, add an independent clause.
   - Trick: Read it aloud. If it feels incomplete, fix it!
2. **FANBOYS Rule**: Use FANBOYS (For, And, Nor, But, Or, Yet, So) to connect independent clauses with a comma.
   - Trick: When in doubt, check if FANBOYS can help join your clauses.
3. **Modifier Placement**: Keep modifiers/appositives beside the words they describe.
   - Trick: Stick to the "close proximity" rule to avoid confusion.
4. **Prepositional Clarity**: Make sure prepositional phrases clearly show where, when, or how something happens.
   - Trick: Visualize the sentence to ensure clarity.

TRIVIA CORNER

- **Longest Sentence:** *The longest sentence in literature is found in Victor Hugo's Les Misérables and contains 823 words. It includes many dependent and independent clauses!*

- **Relative Pronouns in Action:** *Who, whom, whose, which, and that are the most common relative pronouns. They're used to introduce relative clauses that give more information about a noun.*

- **Latin Roots:** *The word "clause" comes from the Latin word clausula, meaning "a close" or "conclusion," as clauses often close or complete a thought.*

- **Appositives Go Way Back:** *Since ancient times, appositive phrases, which rename a noun, have been used to clarify meaning. Shakespeare loved using them for character descriptions!*

- **Common Misstep:** *The most frequent mistake with clauses is the comma splice —joining two independent clauses with just a comma. Always use a conjunction or a period to fix this!*

- **Punctuation Mastery:** *A semicolon is like a super-strong comma. It's often used to link two independent clauses that are closely related without a conjunction.*

- **Dangling Modifiers:** *In an amusing error, a dangling modifier once led to this sentence: "Flying over the countryside, the cows could be seen from the airplane." Watch out—cows don't fly!*

- **Clauses Make Complex Sentences:** *Combining independent and dependent clauses can turn simple sentences into complex ones, allowing for more detailed and exciting writing.*

- **Relative Clause Trick:** *Relative clauses are like little bonus details. You can still understand the sentence without them, but they make it more descriptive.*
- **Prepositional Phrase Limits:** *Some sentences have been found to contain as many as five prepositional phrases in a row, which can confuse the reader. Example: In the box on the table in the room under the stairs. Keep them clear!*

⊚ ACTIVITY CORNER 8

ACTIVITY 1: IDENTIFY THE CLAUSE

Instructions: Label each clause as independent or dependent.

1. Although she was late, she still finished her assignment.
2. I went to the store because we needed milk.
3. While the dog barked, the cat stayed calm.
4. We will go to the park after it stops raining.
5. The movie was great, but the ending was confusing.

ACTIVITY 2: FIX THE DANGLING MODIFIER

Instructions: Correct the dangling modifiers in the following sentences.

1. Running across the field, my hat flew off.
2. After studying all night, the test seemed easy.
3. Swimming in the ocean, the waves seemed huge.
4. Looking through the window, the rain poured down.
5. Covered in snow, the trees sparkled in the sunlight.

ACTIVITY 3: COMBINE SENTENCES USING RELATIVE CLAUSES

Instructions: Combine the following sentences using relative pronouns (who, which, that, whose).

1. The girl is my friend. She lives next door.
2. The book was interesting. I read it last night.
3. The car is very fast. He drives it to school.
4. The teacher gave us homework. The homework was difficult.
5. The boy won the race. His shoes were new.

 ACTIVITY CORNER 8

ACTIVITY 4: APPOSITIVE PHRASES

Instructions: Add an appositive phrase to the following sentences.

1. My sister, _____, is coming to visit.
2. The restaurant, _____, has the best pizza in town.
3. My dog, _____, loves playing in the yard.
4. The book, _____, is on the bestseller list.
5. The actor, _____, starred in that movie.

ACTIVITY 5: PREPOSITIONAL PHRASES IN SENTENCES

Instructions: Identify and underline the prepositional phrases in the following sentences.

1. We walked to the park in the afternoon.
2. The cat jumped onto the table and knocked over the glass.
3. I found my keys under the couch after searching everywhere.
4. The flowers in the garden are blooming beautifully.
5. She sat by the window and read her book.

9. Sentence Clarity and Style

Introduction

In this chapter, you will learn how to write clearly and effectively by removing unnecessary words, avoiding clichés and redundancies, varying sentence structures, and using transitions to maintain flow. These skills will assist you in writing more engaging and polished essays, reports, and creative pieces.

Eliminating Wordiness

Wordiness occurs when too many words express an idea that could be said more simply. Clear, concise writing keeps readers' attention and communicates your ideas directly.

Key Strategies:

- Cut unnecessary words: Phrases like "to" can be shortened to "to."
- To avoid redundancy, Eliminate words that repeat meanings, like "completely finished" (just use "finished").

Examples of Wordiness and Conciseness:

Wordy Sentence	Concise Version
The reason why I left early was because I felt sick.	I left early because I felt sick.
In order to be successful, it is necessary to work hard.	To succeed, you need to work hard.
At this point in time, we are currently reviewing it.	We are reviewing it now.

Avoiding Clichés and Redundancies :

Clichés are overused expressions that have lost their impact. Redundancies involve using multiple words that mean the same thing, unnecessarily repeating the idea.

Common Clichés:

- "Better late than never"
- "The ball is in your court."
- "A blessing in disguise"

Instead of using these phrases, I encourage you to think of original ways to express your ideas. For example:

- Instead of "Better late than never," say, "It's better to be late than not arrive at all."

Examples of Redundancies:

Redundant Phrase	Corrected Version
End result	Result
Free gift	Gift
Unexpected surprise	Surprise
Advance planning	Planning
Past history	History

Identify the clichés and redundancies in these sentences and rewrite them:

- After a lot of planning, we received an unexpected surprise.
- She gave me a free gift for my birthday.
- The ball is in your court, so let me know what you decide.

Commonly Misspelled Words :

These are words that are often spelled incorrectly due to tricky letter combinations or irregular spellings.

Incorrect Spelling	Correct Spelling	Trick to Remember
Definately	Definitely	"Definite-ly" is the base word.
Seperate	Separate	There's 'a rat' in 'separate'.
Neccessary	Necessary	One "c" and two "s"s in necessary.
Accomodate	Accommodate	Two "c"s and two "m"s in accommodate.
Recieve	Receive	"i" before "e" except after "c."
Occured	Occurred	Double "c" and double "r."
Wierd	Weird	"Weird" breaks the "i before e" rule.
Untill	Until	Only one "l" in until.
Beleive	Believe	"i" before "e" except after "c."
Committment	Commitment	Only one "t" in commitment.
Tommorrow	Tomorrow	One "m" in tomorrow.
Suprise	Surprise	"Surprise" has "r" after "u."
Foward	Forward	"For-ward" is the base word.
Goverment	Government	Remember the "n" in government.
Independant	Independent	Ends with "ent," not "ant."
Priviledge	Privilege	Only one "d" in privilege.
Publically	Publicly	Only one "l" in publicly.
Restuarant	Restaurant	"Restau-rant" is the base word.
Seperately	Separately	There's 'a rat' in 'separate-ly'.

Improving Sentence Variety :

Please make sure to avoid using the same type of sentence repeatedly, as it can make your writing sound monotonous. Instead, use a variety of sentence structures, such as simple, compound, complex, and compound-complex sentences, to keep your writing interesting and engaging. Varying the structure of your sentences will help maintain your readers' interest and make your writing more dynamic.

Sentence Types:

- Simple Sentence: A single independent clause.
  - Example: The sun set.
- Compound Sentence: Two independent clauses joined by a coordinating conjunction (FANBOYS).
  - Example: The sun set, and the stars appeared.
- Complex Sentence: One independent clause and at least one dependent clause.
  - Example: When the sun set, the stars appeared.
- Compound-Complex Sentence: Two or more independent clauses and at least one dependent clause.
  - Example: When the sun set, the stars appeared, and the moon rose.

Table: Sentence Variety Examples

Sentence Type	Example
Simple	The students studied.
Compound	The students studied, but they didn't finish their homework.
Complex	Although the students studied, they didn't finish their homework.
Compound-Complex	Although they studied, the students didn't finish, but they tried their best.

Transitions and Flow :

Transitions are words or phrases that connect ideas and help your writing flow smoothly. They guide your reader through your arguments or narrative.

Types of Transitions:

- Addition: Furthermore, in addition, also
- Contrast: However on the other hand, nevertheless
- Cause and Effect: Therefore, as a result, consequently
- Conclusion: In conclusion, to sum up, finally

Example of Using Transitions in a Paragraph:

- **Without Transitions,** I woke up late, missed the bus, and arrived late to school.
- **With Transitions**, I woke up late, missed the bus, and arrived late to school.

Table: Transition Types and Examples

Transition Type	Examples
Addition	Also, furthermore, in addition
Contrast	However, on the other hand, but
Cause and Effect	Therefore, as a result, consequently
Conclusion	In conclusion, to sum up, finally

Common Mistakes and How to Avoid Them

Mistake	Solution	Tip/Trick
Wordiness: Using too many unnecessary words	Cut down on extra words. Use precise language.	Focus on the main idea and eliminate any extra phrases.
Clichés: Overusing common phrases	Think of fresh, original ways to express your thoughts.	Replace clichés with more specific, personal descriptions.
Lack of sentence variety	Use a mix of simple, compound, complex, and compound-complex sentences to add variety.	Read your writing aloud to hear the rhythm and flow.
Poor transitions	Use transition words to connect ideas and guide your reader through your writing.	Use transitions at the beginning of sentences for clarity.
Redundancy: Repeating the same meaning twice	Eliminate one of the words or phrases if they mean the same thing.	Ask: Does one word already cover the meaning?

TRIVIA CORNER

1. A Wordy Challenge: Pneumonoultramicroscopicsilicovolcanoconiosis, a lung disease caused by inhaling very fine silicate dust, is the longest word in the English dictionary, clocking in at 45 letters. Can you say it five times fast?

2. The Minimalist Sentence: The shortest complete sentence in English is "I am," consisting of just two words: a subject and a verb. It proves that sometimes, less is more.

3. Shakespeare's Wordsmithing: William Shakespeare was a master of language, inventing over 1,700 words that we still use today, including "eyeball," "fashionable," and "lonely."

4. The Origin of Clichés: The term "cliché" comes from the French word for "stereotype." It originally referred to the sound a printing press made when it produced a worn-out plate.

5. Jargon: The Language of Experts: Jargon is a specialized language used by a particular group or profession. While it can be useful for communicating with peers, overuse can make writing unclear to a wider audience.

6. Transitions: The Glue of Writing: Transition words and phrases act as connectors, linking ideas together smoothly. They help your writing flow and make it easier to follow.

7. Sentence Variety: Spice Up Your Writing: Mixing up sentence lengths and structures can make your writing more engaging. Short sentences can create a sense of urgency, while longer ones can provide more detail.

8. Shakespeare's Famous Soliloquy: One of the most famous sentences in literature, "To be or not to be," is a simple declarative sentence. It shows that even complex ideas can be expressed in a straightforward way.

9. Redundancy: A Wordy Habit: Redundancy occurs when you use unnecessary words or phrases. Common examples include "close proximity," "end result," and "ATM machine" (since "ATM" already stands for "Automated Teller Machine").

10. The First Transition Word: The earliest recorded use of a transition word in its modern sense dates back to the 15th century. The word was "moreover," which was used in legal documents to add additional points.

ACTIVITY CORNER 9

Activity 1: Eliminate Wordiness

Instructions: Below are sentences with unnecessary words. Rewrite each sentence to make it more concise without changing the meaning.

1. *Due to the fact that she was late, she missed the beginning of the class.*
2. *In the event that it rains tomorrow, the game will be canceled.*
3. *He made the decision to go to the mall with his friends.*
4. *The reason why the team lost was because they weren't prepared.*
5. *She gave a brief summary of the entire project.*

Activity 2: Avoiding Clichés

Instructions: Clichés are overused phrases that weaken writing. Rewrite the following sentences by replacing the clichés with fresh language.

1. *At the end of the day, we all just want to succeed.*
2. *He worked hard, but it was an uphill battle.*
3. *Actions speak louder than words, so she decided to volunteer.*
4. *Time will tell if the new policy works.*
5. *She was as quiet as a mouse during the meeting.*

Activity 3 : Sentence Variety Challenge

Instructions: Rewrite the following paragraph, varying the sentence structure to make it more engaging. Try using a mix of simple, compound, and complex sentences.

"The students arrived at the park. They saw the large picnic area. The weather was sunny. Everyone brought food to share. They set up a volleyball net and started playing."

 ACTIVITY CORNER 9

Activity 4 : Transitions and Flow

Instructions: Fill in the blanks with the most appropriate transition word to improve the flow of the paragraph.

Options: **however, therefore, meanwhile, for example, consequently**

"The weather forecast predicted rain; ____, we decided to postpone the event. ____, we made sure to inform everyone. ____, the weather cleared up unexpectedly. ____, we will still host the event next week. ____, we might have learned something about trusting weather forecasts."

Activity 5 : Redundancy Hunt

Instructions: Read the following sentences. Identify the redundant words or phrases, and rewrite the sentences without the redundancies.

1. *The meeting began at 10 a.m. in the morning.*
2. *He added an extra bonus to their paychecks.*
3. *She entered the room, which was filled with furniture.*
4. *The final outcome of the race was unexpected.*
5. *The reason he left was because he was feeling sick.*

10. Common Grammatical Mistakes

Grammar mistakes can easily sneak into our writing, causing confusion and making it harder for others to understand what we mean. This chapter will help you identify and fix common grammar errors to improve sentence clarity and polish your writing. We'll explore double negatives, commonly confused words, subject and object pronouns, and common spelling and grammar mistakes.

Double Negatives

A double negative occurs when two negative words are used in the same sentence. This can lead to confusion because the two negatives can cancel each other out, resulting in a positive meaning that wasn't intended.

Example of a Double Negative:

- **Incorrect:** I don't need any help with this homework.
  - This sentence uses two negatives: "don't" and "no." It unintentionally suggests that the speaker does need help.
- **Correct**: I don't need any help with this homework.
  - This version uses only one negative word ("don't"), which makes the sentence clear.

Table: Common Double Negatives and Their Corrections

Incorrect	Correct
I don't have no time.	I don't have any time.
She didn't say nothing.	She didn't say anything.
We can't find no solution.	We can't find a solution.
He wasn't going nowhere.	He wasn't going anywhere.
They didn't do nothing.	They didn't do anything.

Confusing Words and Homophones

Homophones are words that sound the same but have different meanings and spellings. Many students often mix up these words, which can alter the meaning of a sentence and result in errors. Let's explore some common pairs.

Common Homophones Table

Word Pair	Definition	Example
There	Refers to a place.	The book is there on the table.
Their	Shows possession.	It's their decision to make.
They're	Contraction of "they are."	They're going to the park.
Affect	A verb, meaning to influence.	The bad weather affects my mood.
Effect	A noun, meaning a result.	The effect of the storm was severe.
Your	Shows possession.	Is this your book?
You're	Contraction of "you are."	You're going to love this movie.
It's	Contraction of "it is."	It's raining outside.
Its	Shows possession.	The cat licked its paw.
Lose	A verb, meaning to misplace.	Don't lose your phone.
Loose	An adjective, meaning not tight.	This shirt is too loose.

Tricks for Confusing Words:

- There, Their, They're:

  - Use there for location (over there), their for possession (their house), and they're for "they are" (they're going).

- Affect vs. Effect:

  - Affect is an action (a verb); it means to change or influence. Effect is a result (a noun). Remember: Affect is an Action, Effect is an End result.

Subject and Object Pronouns

Pronouns replace nouns to avoid repetition. It's essential to choose the correct pronoun depending on whether it's the subject or object in the sentence.

Subject Pronouns:

Used when the pronoun is the subject of the sentence (the "doer" of the action).

- **Subject Pronouns:** I, you, he, she, it, we, they.
- **Example**: She runs every morning.

Object Pronouns:

Used when the pronoun is the object of the sentence (the receiver of the action).

- **Object Pronouns**: me, you, him, her, it, us, them.
- **Example:** The coach gave him the trophy.

Table: Subject vs. Object Pronouns

Pronoun Type	Pronouns	Example Sentence
Subject Pronouns	I, you, he, she, it, we, they	He is the team captain.
Object Pronouns	me, you, him, her, it, us, them	The teacher gave us homework.

Trick to Remember:

- If you're unsure, ask who is doing the action (use a subject pronoun) and who is receiving it (use an object pronoun). For example, in "He gave her the book," "he" is doing the action (giving), so "he" is the subject, while "her" receives the book, so "her" is the object.

Common Spelling and Grammar Mistakes

Spelling and grammar mistakes happen often, but they're easy to fix once you know what to look for. Below are some frequently made errors.

Common Grammar Mistakes

Mistake	Correct Version	Explanation
Your going to love this movie.	You're going to love this movie.	"You're" is a contraction for "you are."
The dog wagged it's tail.	The dog wagged its tail.	"Its" shows possession. "It's" means "it is."
I will except your apology.	I will accept your apology.	"Accept" means to receive; "except" means to exclude.
The dress is to small.	The dress is too small.	"Too" means "also" or "very"; "to" is a preposition.

Common Mistakes and Solutions Table

Mistake	Corrected Sentence	Trick
I don't want none.	I don't want any.	Use only one negative word.
He didn't do nothing.	He didn't do anything.	Replace "nothing" with "anything."
Its raining outside.	It's raining outside.	"It's" = it is.
We went to there house.	We went to their house.	"Their" shows possession.
You should of studied.	You should have studied.	"Should of" is incorrect—use "should have."

Sentence Variety Example :

- **Simple Sentence**: I ran to the store.
- **Compound Sentence**: I ran to the store, and I bought a drink.
- **Complex Sentence**: Although I was tired, I ran to the store.
- **Compound-Complex Sentence**: I ran to the store, but I was late, because my bike broke.

Tips for Avoiding Common Mistakes

1. **Double Negative Test:**
   - Tip: If your sentence feels awkward or confusing, check if you've used two negative words. Remove one to make the sentence clear.
2. **Homophone Trick:**
   - Tip: To avoid mixing up homophones, say the sentence aloud or think about the meaning of each word in context. For example, if it's a location, use "there."
3. **Pronoun Placement:**
   - Tip: Remove extra details to isolate the pronoun. For example, in the sentence "John and me went to the store," simplify it to "Me went to the store" and you'll see the mistake—it should be "I went to the store."

TRIVIA CORNER

- **Double Negatives** : Using two negatives in a sentence can accidentally create a positive meaning. For example, "I don't need no help" means "I do need help."

- **"Affect" vs. "Effect"**: While "effect" is typically a noun meaning "result," "affect" can be both a verb meaning "to influence" and a noun meaning "emotion."

- **Common Word Pairs**: English has many confusing word pairs, like "there/their/they're," "your/you're," and "its/it's."

- **Homophones:** Words that sound the same but have different meanings (homophones) are a common source of spelling errors.

- **Pronoun Variation:** Pronouns can change form based on the language and the speaker's relationship to the listener. For example, in Japanese, pronouns can vary based on social status.

- **"Affect" and "Effect" History:** The confusion between "affect" and "effect" has a long history, dating back to Shakespeare's time.

- **Longest Sentence:** James Joyce's novel "Ulysses" contains a famously long sentence, known as the "Finnegan's Wake sentence."

- **Double Negatives in Music:** Double negatives are often used in music for emphasis and lyrical effect, as seen in songs like "I Can't Get No Satisfaction."

- **Googled Grammar Questions:** While "its" vs. "it's" is a common grammar question, it's difficult to confirm if it's the most Googled.

- **Technology and Spelling**: The rise of technology, including texting and social media, has influenced language usage, including spelling and grammar.

ACTIVITY CORNER 10

ACTIVITY 1: SPOT THE DOUBLE NEGATIVES

Instructions: Identify and correct the double negatives in the following sentences.

1. I don't have no idea what's going on.
2. She didn't say nothing about the project.
3. They can't find nobody to help them.
4. We didn't do nothing wrong.
5. He doesn't need no help with his homework.

ACTIVITY 2: HOMOPHONE FILL-IN-THE-BLANKS

Instructions: Fill in the blanks with the correct homophone.

1. I can't believe you're already _____ (there/their/they're).
2. She's going to _____ (accept/except) the award on behalf of her team.
3. I need to return this book to _____ (its/it's) rightful owner.
4. Please tell me how this will _____ (affect/effect) our plans.
5. He said he would meet us over _____ (hear/here).

ACTIVITY 3: CORRECT THE PRONOUNS

Instructions: Choose the correct pronoun (subject or object) to complete the sentences.

1. _____ (He/Him) and I went to the concert together.
2. The teacher gave _____ (she/her) extra credit for the project.
3. It was _____ (I/me) who finished the homework first.
4. _____ (They/Them) told us about the new movie.
5. I can't wait to see _____ (he/him) next week.

ACTIVITY 4: FIX THE CONFUSING WORDS

Instructions: Correct the confusing word choices in the following sentences.

1. The news had a big affect on everyone.
2. It's time to get their homework done.
3. She can't find her phone anywhere; she must of left it at home.
4. We'll except any reasonable offer.
5. Their coming over for dinner tonight.

ACTIVITY CORNER 1

Activity 1: Identify the Parts of Speech

Answer Key:
1. After – Preposition
2. school – Noun
3. Tim – Noun
4. quickly – Adverb
5. ran – Verb
6. to – Preposition
7. the – Article (Adjective)
8. park – Noun
9. and – Conjunction
10. played – Verb
11. soccer – Noun
12. with – Preposition
13. his – Pronoun
14. friends – Noun

Activity 2: Correct the Common Grammar Errors

Answer Key:
1. My friend and I are going to the mall.
2. She doesn't like broccoli.
3. They were late to class yesterday.
4. He could have gone to the game but chose to stay home.

Activity 3: Fix the Sentence for Clarity

Answer Key:
"The trees looked beautiful as I was running through the park."

Activity 4: Match the Grammar Component

Answer Key:

1. Noun – c. Cat
2. Verb – e. Ran
3. Adjective – d. Beautiful
4. Adverb – a. Quickly
5. Pronoun – f. She
6. Preposition – g. With
7. Conjunction – h. And
8. Article – b. The

Activity 5: SAT/ACT Grammar Practice

Answer Key:

1. are (The subject closest to the verb is plural, so the verb must agree.)
2. has (Everyone is a singular indefinite pronoun, so the verb must be singular.)
3. were (The subject closest to the verb is plural, so the verb must agree.)
4. is (Each is a singular pronoun, so the verb must be singular.)

ACTIVITY CORNER 2

Activity 1: Identifying Types of Nouns

Answers:

1. *Collective*
2. *Proper*
3. *Abstract*
4. *Collective*
5. *Proper*

Activity 2: Pronoun-Antecedent Agreement

Answers:
1. his or her
2. its
3. his
4. his or her
5. its

Activity Corner 3: Spelling Bee Practice

Answers:
1. walked, cooked
2. will have finished
3. was studying, answered
4. had read, watched
5. will go, have

Activity 4: Identifying Adjectives and Adverbs

Answers:

1. *Adjective (happy)*
2. *Adverb (beautifully)*
3. *Adjective (large), Adverb (loudly)*
4. *Adverb (early)*
5. *Adverb (quietly)*

Activity 5: Conjunctions and Prepositions

Answers:

1. under
2. and
3. and
4. but
5. on

ACTIVITY CORNER 3

Activity 1: Identifying Sentence Types

Answers:

1. *Simple*
2. *Complex*
3. *Compound*
4. *Simple*
5. *Complex*

Activity 2: Subject-Verb Agreement Fix

Answers:
1. The group of students is going to the library.
2. Every dog and cat likes to sleep in the sun.
3. Neither the teacher nor the students were prepared for the surprise quiz.
4. The books on the shelf need to be organized.
5. Either my brother or my parents are driving me to school today.

Activity Corner 3: Sentence Fragment or Complete Sentence?

Answers:
1. Fragment – After the concert ended, we went home.
2. Complete Sentence
3. Fragment – Because it was raining, we stayed indoors.
4. Complete Sentence
5. Fragment – He was running down the street.

Activity 4: Correcting Run-on Sentences

Answers:

1. *She loves reading, and she goes to the library every week.*
2. *The sun is shining; the weather is perfect for a picnic.*
3. *I studied all night, but I still didn't pass the test.*
4. *He cooked dinner, and it tasted amazing.*
5. *The car broke down, so we had to walk home.*

Activity 5: Parallel Structure Check

Answers:

1. He likes swimming, running, and biking.
2. The teacher told us to read the book, take notes, and review for the test.
3. Correct
4. The job requires attention to detail, creativity, and punctuality.
5. Correct

ACTIVITY CORNER 4

ACTIVITY 1: FIX THE PUNCTUATION

Answer Key:
1. "Where are you going tomorrow?" asked Jessica.
2. The students' books were all over the floor.
3. He didn't know whether to laugh, cry, or shout.
4. Can I borrow your pen for a minute?
5. We will visit Paris, London, and Rome on our trip.

ACTIVITY 2: INSERT THE COMMAS

Answer Key:
1. My favorite colors are red, blue, green, and yellow.
2. Before leaving, make sure you have your keys.
3. The cake, which was delicious, was baked by my mom.
4. Sarah, John, and Emily went to the movies last night.
5. After the meeting, we went out for coffee.

ACTIVITY 3: SEMICOLONS AND COLONS PRACTICE

Answer Key:
1. I have three things to buy: eggs, milk, and bread.
2. It was raining heavily; I decided to stay indoors.
3. The meeting starts at 9:00; please be on time.
4. She had one goal: to win the race.
5. I love traveling; I've been to Italy, Spain, and Greece.

ACTIVITY 4: QUOTATION MARKS IN DIALOGUE

Answer Key:
1. Jessica said, "I can't wait for summer break."
2. Can you believe he just said, "I'm not going to the party"?
3. The teacher told us, "Finish your homework tonight."
4. "Is the answer really true?" she asked.
5. I read the short story "The Lottery" for class.

ACTIVITY 5 : APOSTROPHE USAGE

Answer Key:
1. The cat's toys were scattered all over the house.
2. It's raining outside, so don't forget your umbrella.
3. The girls' locker room is on the left.
4. The children's books were organized by genre.
5. I can't believe it's already time for the exam.

ACTIVITY CORNER 5

Activity 1: Pronoun Identification Quiz

Answers:
1. She – personal pronoun
2. This – demonstrative pronoun
3. Who – relative pronoun
4. They – personal pronoun
5. Nobody – indefinite pronoun

Activity 2: Correct the Vague Pronoun Reference

1. When Alex spoke to Chris, Alex was confused.
2. Sarah gave the book to Emily, and Emily put it on the shelf.
3. After the teacher handed the paper to James, James lost it.
4. When John helped Michael, Michael thanked him.
5. The dog chased the cat, and the cat ran into the yard.

Activity 3: Pronoun-Antecedent Agreement Matching

Answers:
1. His – D. The boys
2. Their – A. The students
3. Her – B. Emily
4. Its – C. The dog

Activity 4 : Pronoun Case Quiz

Answers:
1. me
2. he
3. my
4. me
5. We

Activity 5: Fill in the Blanks with the Correct Pronoun

Answers:
1. Answers:
2. her
3. their
4. his or her
5. their
6. his or her

107

ACTIVITY CORNER 5

Activity 5 : Pronoun Identification Quiz

Answers:
1. She – personal pronoun
2. This – demonstrative pronoun
3. Who – relative pronoun
4. They – personal pronoun
5. Nobody – indefinite pronoun

Activity 2: Correct the Vague Pronoun Reference

1. When Alex spoke to Chris, Alex was confused.
2. Sarah gave the book to Emily, and Emily put it on the shelf.
3. After the teacher handed the paper to James, James lost it.
4. When John helped Michael, Michael thanked him.
5. The dog chased the cat, and the cat ran into the yard.

Activity 3: Pronoun-Antecedent Agreement Matching

Answers:
1. His – D. The boys
2. Their – A. The students
3. Her – B. Emily
4. Its – C. The dog

Activity 4 : Pronoun Case Quiz

Answers:
1. me
2. he
3. my
4. me
5. We

ACTIVITY CORNER 6

ACTIVITY 1: IDENTIFY THE VERB TENSE

Answer:

1. Present perfect
2. Future progressive
3. Past progressive
4. Simple present
5. Future perfect

ACTIVITY 2 : CORRECT THE TENSE SHIFT

Answers:

1. She walked into the room and saw her friend.
2. I was watching TV when my phone rang.
3. They visited us last week and had a great time.
4. He ate dinner and then washed the dishes.
5. The dog barked loudly as the mailman approached.

ACTIVITY 3 : ACTIVE VS. PASSIVE VOICE

Answers:

1. John kicked the ball.
2. The students completed the homework.
3. Sarah baked the cake.
4. The teacher wrote the letter.
5. The team finished the project.

ACTIVITY 4 :FILL IN THE IRREGULAR VERB

Answers:

1. went
2. eaten
3. saw
4. done
5. ran

ACTIVITY 5 : MATCH THE TENSE TO THE SENTENCE

Answers:

1. I have lived here for ten years. – Present perfect
2. She was walking to school when it started raining. – Past progressive
3. They will travel to Paris next year. – Future simple
4. He had already left when they arrived. – Past perfect
5. We are studying for the test right now. – Present progressive

ACTIVITY CORNER 7

ACTIVITY 1: IDENTIFY THE MODIFIER

Answers:

1. energetic (adjective), happily (adverb)
2. quickly (adverb)
3. old (adjective), gently (adverb)
4. large (adjective), colorful (adjective)
5. carefully (adverb)

ACTIVITY 2 : FIX THE MISPLACED MODIFIERS

Answers:

1. The teacher, with a smile, handed out tests to the students.
2. Looking out the window, she saw a bird with a bright red beak.
3. I ordered the pizza covered in cheese.
4. Carrying their backpacks, the kids walked home singing loudly.
5. He ate nearly all the ice cream in the fridge.

ACTIVITY 3 : CORRECT THE DANGLING MODIFIERS

Answers:

1. After eating lunch, I cleaned the dishes.
2. While driving home, I noticed the weather turned stormy.
3. Looking out of the window, I saw a breathtaking view.
4. Walking down the street, I saw the trees seemed to be dancing.
5. By working hard, we achieved success.

ACTIVITY CORNER 7

ACTIVITY 4 : COMPARATIVES AND SUPERLATIVES

Answers:

1. John is taller than Mark, but Sam is the tallest in the class.
2. This book is more interesting than the one I read last week.
3. Of all my friends, Sarah is the funniest.
4. Today's weather is worse than yesterday.
5. Out of all the players, Leo is the be

ACTIVITY 5 : ADJECTIVES OR ADVERBS?

Answers:

1. loudly
2. happy
3. beautifully
4. nice
5. carefully

ACTIVITY CORNER 8

ACTIVITY 1: IDENTIFY THE CLAUSE

1. Dependent: Although she was late | Independent: She still finished her assignment.
2. Independent: I went to the store | Dependent: Because we needed milk.
3. Dependent: While the dog barked | Independent: The cat stayed calm.
4. Independent: We will go to the park | Dependent: After it stops raining.
5. Independent: The movie was great | Independent: The ending was confusing.

ACTIVITY 2 : FIX THE DANGLING MODIFIER

1. Running across the field, I lost my hat.
2. After studying all night, I found the test easy.
3. Swimming in the ocean, we noticed the waves were huge.
4. Looking through the window, I watched as the rain poured down.
5. Covered in snow, the trees sparkled in the sunlight.

ACTIVITY 3 : COMBINE SENTENCES USING RELATIVE CLAUSES

1. The girl who lives next door is my friend.
2. The book that I read last night was interesting.
3. The car which he drives to school is very fast.
4. The homework that the teacher gave us was difficult.
5. The boy whose shoes were new won the race.

ACTIVITY 4 : APPOSITIVE PHRASES

1. My sister, a talented artist, is coming to visit.
2. The restaurant, a cozy Italian spot, has the best pizza in town.
3. My dog, a playful golden retriever, loves playing in the yard.
4. The book, a thrilling mystery novel, is on the bestseller list.
5. The actor, a Hollywood star, starred in that movie.

ACTIVITY 4 : PREPOSITIONAL PHRASES IN SENTENCES

1. We walked to the park in the afternoon.
2. The cat jumped onto the table and knocked over the glass.
3. I found my keys under the couch after searching everywhere.
4. The flowers in the garden are blooming beautifully.
5. She sat by the window and read her book.

ACTIVITY CORNER 9

ACTIVITY 1: ELIMINATE WORDINESS

Answers:

1. Since she was late, she missed the beginning of the class.
2. If it rains tomorrow, the game will be canceled.
3. He decided to go to the mall with his friends.
4. The team lost because they weren't prepared.
5. She summarized the entire project.

ACTIVITY 2 : AVOIDING CLICHÉS

Answers:

1. I will definitely go to the party.
2. She is a very intelligent student.
3. Please separate the laundry into different piles.
4. He received a gift from his friend.
5. It is necessary to bring your own stationery.
6. The accommodations were very comfortable.
7. She was embarrassed by her mistake.
8. The weird noise scared the children.
9. He doesn't know whether to laugh or cry.
10. I received an invitation to the event.

ACTIVITY 3: SENTENCE VARIETY CHALLENGE

Sample Answer: *The students arrived at the park and noticed the large picnic area. The weather was sunny, which put everyone in a great mood. While some students brought food to share, others set up a volleyball net and started playing. It was a perfect day for outdoor fun.*

ACTIVITY 4 : TRANSITIONS AND FLOW

Answers:

1. however
2. therefore
3. meanwhile
4. consequently
5. for example

ACTIVITY 5 : REDUNDANCY HUNT

Answers:

1. The meeting began at 10 a.m.
2. He added a bonus to their paychecks.
3. She entered the room, which was filled with furniture.
4. The outcome of the race was unexpected.
5. He left because he was feeling sick.

ACTIVITY CORNER 10

ACTIVITY 1: SPOT THE DOUBLE NEGATIVES

Answers:

1. I don't have any idea what's going on.
2. She didn't say anything about the project.
3. They can't find anybody to help them.
4. We didn't do anything wrong.
5. He doesn't need any help with his homework.

ACTIVITY 2 : HOMOPHONE FILL-IN-THE-BLANKS

Answers:

1. they're
2. accept
3. its
4. affect
5. here

ACTIVITY 3: CORRECT THE PRONOUNS

Answers:

1. He
2. her
3. I
4. They
5. him

ACTIVITY 4 : FIX THE CONFUSING WORDS

Answers:

1. The news had a big effect on everyone.
2. It's time to get their homework done.
3. She can't find her phone anywhere; she must have left it at home.
4. We'll accept any reasonable offer.
5. They're coming over for dinner tonight.

11. SAT/ACT - Types of
Grammar Questions

TYPES OF QUESTIONS

Question Type	Description	Example Sentence	Explanation
Identifying Errors	Identify any grammatical errors in underlined portions of a sentence.	"The students are excited about their upcoming trip to the museum."	No error in the word "trip."
Improving Sentences	Choose the best way to express an idea, focusing on clarity, conciseness, or grammar.	"Because of the bad weather, the game was postponed." → "Due to the inclement weather, the game was rescheduled."	The second option is more concise and formal.
Revising Sentences	Identify and correct grammatical errors or awkward phrasing.	"Me and my friend went to the store." → "My friend and I went to the store."	Correct pronoun usage: "My friend and I."
Sentence Completion	Choose the correct word or phrase to grammatically and logically complete a sentence.	"The cat is ___ sleeping on the couch." → "peacefully"	"Peacefully" completes the sentence logically.

COMMON ERRORS IN IDENTIFYING ERRORS QUESTIONS

Sentence	Error Found	Corrected Sentence
The dog wagged it's tail.	it's (possessive error)	The dog wagged its tail.
I seen the movie yesterday.	seen (verb tense error)	I saw the movie yesterday.
Neither John nor Mary are going to the party.	are (subject-verb agreement)	Neither John nor Mary is going to the party.
The team have won the match.	have (subject-verb agreement)	The team has won the match.
He should of come earlier.	of (wrong word)	He should have come earlier.

EXAMPLES OF IMPROVING SENTENCES

Original Sentence	Improved Sentence	Why It's Better
The book was very interesting, and I enjoyed reading it.	I found the book to be very interesting and enjoyable.	More concise and natural.
We are going to the store because we need milk.	We need milk, so we are going to the store.	More direct and to the point.
The cake tasted very delicious.	The cake was delicious.	"Very delicious" is redundant.
She quickly ran across the street.	She sprinted across the street.	Stronger verb eliminates the need for "quickly."
The meeting is scheduled for 3 p.m. in the afternoon.	The meeting is scheduled for 3 p.m.	"In the afternoon" is redundant with "3 p.m."

EXAMPLES OF REVISING SENTENCES

Original Sentence	Correct Sentence	Error Type
Me and my friend went to the store.	My friend and I went to the store.	Pronoun usage
The cake tasted very delicious.	The cake was delicious.	Redundancy
Him and her are going to the movies.	He and she are going to the movies.	Pronoun usage
The teacher, who she is very nice, helped us.	The teacher, who is very nice, helped us.	Unnecessary pronoun
He ran down the street quickly.	He quickly ran down the street.	Modifier placement

EXAMPLES OF SENTENCE COMPLETION

Sentence	Correct Answer	Explanation
I am ___ excited to go to the party.	very	"Very" modifies "excited" correctly.
The book was ___ interesting.	quite	"Quite" intensifies "interesting."
The dog is ___ barking in the yard.	loudly	"Loudly" describes how the dog is barking.
She walked ___ to the park.	quickly	"Quickly" describes how she walked.
The teacher is ___ explaining the concept.	clearly	"Clearly" describes how the teacher explains the concept.

TIPS FOR SUCCESS

Strategy	Description
Know the Rules	Understand key grammar rules like subject-verb agreement, pronouns, and tenses.
Eliminate Incorrect Choices	Narrow down your options by eliminating answers that contain clear mistakes.
Practice Regularly	Regular practice improves your ability to spot grammar errors.
Read Critically	Pay attention to grammar and sentence structure in well-written texts.
Look for Distractors	Be aware of incorrect choices designed to confuse you.
Stay Calm and Focused	Take your time and avoid rushing through the questions.

COMMON MISTAKES AND HOW TO FIX THEM

Common Mistake	Error Explanation	How to Fix It
It's vs. Its	It's = "it is"; Its = possessive.	Use its for possession, it's for "it is."
Their, They're, There	Their = possession; they're = "they are"; there = place.	Check the context to determine the correct form.
Misplaced Modifiers	Modifier is in the wrong place in the sentence.	Place the modifier next to the word it describes.
Subject-Verb Agreement	The verb does not match the subject in number.	Ensure singular subjects have singular verbs and plural subjects have plural verbs.
Double Negatives	Two negatives cancel each other out.	Avoid using two negative words in the same sentence.

CONCLUSION

Congratulations on completing the High School Grammar Workbook Grade 9-12: Grammar Practice Workbook! By working through the chapters, you've built a strong grammar foundation to improve your writing and boost your confidence in standardized tests like the SAT, ACT, and high school exams. In standardized tests like the SAT, ACT, and high school exams.

Key Takeaways:

- Understanding Parts of Speech: You learned how nouns, verbs, adjectives, adverbs, conjunctions, and prepositions function in sentences, allowing you to write precisely and clearly.
- Mastering Sentence Structure: You know how to craft simple, compound, and complex sentences while avoiding fragments and run-ons. You've also learned the importance of subject-verb agreement and parallel structure.
- Punctuation and Capitalization: You've gained skills that will elevate your writing from mastering the proper use of commas and semicolons to understanding the rules for quotation marks and apostrophes.
- Pronouns and Verb Tenses: Correct pronoun usage and consistent verb tense are vital to clear communication. You've learned to avoid vague pronoun references and mastered irregular verb forms.
- Modifiers and Clauses: You've honed your ability to use modifiers correctly and identified how clauses and phrases help create complex and engaging sentences.
- Sentence Clarity and Style: With skills to eliminate wordiness, avoid clichés, and improve sentence variety, you are now capable of writing clear and effective prose.
- Common Grammar Pitfalls: You've tackled frequent errors like double negatives, confusing words, and homophones, ensuring your writing is grammatically sound.

Looking Forward:

The knowledge and practice you've gained from this workbook are tools that will serve you in every writing task, whether you are drafting essays, writing emails, or preparing for exams. Remember, strong grammar skills are the backbone of excellent communication. Mastering them will set you apart in your academic and professional journey.

CONCLUSION

Keep Practicing:

Grammar is a skill that improves with consistent practice. Continue to apply what you've learned, and don't hesitate to revisit this workbook when you need a refresher. The exercises and explanations will always help you strengthen your knowledge of grammar.

Final Thought:

Grammar may seem like a set of rigid rules, but it's the foundation for creative, clear, and compelling expression. Mastering grammar opens doors to better communication, higher test scores, and tremendous success in every area of your life.

Best of luck on your writing journey, and remember that every word matters!

We'd Love Your Feedback!

Please let us know how we're doing by leaving us a review.

APPENDIX : ADDITIONAL RESOURCES

Recommended Books

Book Title	Author	Description	Level
The Elements of Style	William Strunk Jr. & E.B. White	A classic guide to grammar, style, and writing clarity. Provides essential rules of usage and writing tips.	Beginner to Advanced
Grammar Girl's Quick and Dirty Tips for Better Writing	Mignon Fogarty	Easy-to-follow tips on improving grammar, punctuation, and usage. Includes common grammar pitfalls and solutions.	Intermediate
English Grammar in Use	Raymond Murphy	A comprehensive grammar reference book with detailed explanations and exercises to solidify understanding. Suitable for both self-study and classroom use.	Beginner to Intermediate
Woe Is I: The Grammarphobe's Guide to Better English in Plain English	Patricia T. O'Conner	A witty and accessible guide that simplifies grammar rules for everyday use. Ideal for students who want a less formal approach to learning.	Intermediate
The Blue Book of Grammar and Punctuation	Jane Straus	Covers essential grammar and punctuation rules with straightforward explanations and plenty of practice questions.	All Levels

Recommended Websites

Website	URL	Description	Best For
Purdue Online Writing Lab (OWL)	https://owl.purdue.edu	Offers detailed grammar rules, writing tips, and exercises. A comprehensive resource for grammar, punctuation, and style guides.	High school students, SAT/ACT prep
Grammarly Blog	https://www.grammarly.com/blog	Provides grammar tips, writing advice, and explanations of common writing mistakes. Includes interactive tools for correcting grammar in real-time.	All levels
Khan Academy SAT Grammar	https://www.khanacademy.org	Offers free grammar lessons and SAT preparation materials. The grammar section focuses on sentence structure, punctuation, and verb tenses.	SAT/ACT test preparation
Grammar Monster	https://www.grammar-monster.com	Features a wide range of grammar lessons, quizzes, and interactive exercises for all levels.	General grammar improvement
NoRedInk	https://www.noredink.com	Provides personalized grammar exercises, quizzes, and writing prompts. Great for targeted grammar practice.	High school students

APPENDIX- 1 : ADDITIONAL RESOURCES

Recommended YT/ Apps

App/YouTube Channel	Platform	Description	Best For
Grammarly	App (iOS/Android), Website	A popular app that provides grammar checks, punctuation suggestions, and style improvements in real-time for both writing and editing.	All levels
Duolingo English	App (iOS/Android)	Known for language learning, Duolingo also includes grammar lessons to help with sentence structure and verb usage in English.	Beginner to Intermediate
Learn English Grammar (British Council)	App (iOS/Android)	An interactive app that offers grammar lessons and quizzes. Focuses on common grammar points tested in exams.	All levels
Khan Academy SAT Prep (Grammar)	YouTube	Free video tutorials covering SAT-specific grammar questions, including sentence structure, punctuation, and subject-verb agreement.	SAT/ACT test preparation
CrashCourse English	YouTube	Offers engaging grammar lessons and writing tutorials, covering basic to advanced concepts with fun and educational videos.	High school students
English with Lucy	YouTube	Provides grammar tips, writing strategies, and common grammar mistakes. Lucy's engaging teaching style makes learning grammar fun and practical.	Intermediate to Advanced

We'd Love Your Feedback!

Please let us know how we're doing by leaving us a review.

YOUNG WRITER SERIES - DR. FANATOMY

THE 5-PARAGRAPH ESSAY MASTERY
A Teen Writer's Workbook

A WORKBOOK FOR TEENS, PROVIDING STEP-BY-STEP GUIDANCE ON HOW TO WRITE A 5-PARAGRAPH ESSAY

DR. FANATOMY

READING COMPREHENSION HIGH SCHOOL

READING COMPREHENSION GRADE 9-12 WORKBOOK : ACHIEVE HIGHER TEST SCORES WITH INTERACTIVE EXERCISES

DR. FANATOMY

HIGH SCHOOL SPELLING & VOCABULARY WORKBOOK

ACHIEVE HIGHER TEST SCORES WITH INTERACTIVE EXERCISES: VOCABULARY AND SPELLING HIGH SCHOOL WORKBOOK FOR GRADES 9-10

DR. FANATOMY

PARAGRAPH WRITING & EDITING WORKBOOK FOR HIGH SCHOOL

A Paragraph Writing Workbook for Teens Guiding them How to write an Awesome Paragraph

DR. FANATOMY

Made in the USA
Middletown, DE
30 December 2024